THE
MINDFULNESS
Rx

Mindful prescription for stress, anxiety, ADHD, pain, PTSD,
addictions, depression, loneliness, insomnia

VALERIE FOSTER
BILL VAN OLLEFEN

Health issues are complex and this book and any suggestions, programs or ideas are not intended to replace the advice of any trained medical professional. Anything that impacts another's health requires medical supervision.

The authors' roles are meant to educate, not to medically assess or offer any personal medical advice. Check with your medical provider before adopting any of the recommendations put forth in this book.

The authors disclaim any liability arising directly or indirectly from the use of this book.

Copyright © 2020 by Valerie Foster and Bill Van Ollefen. All rights reserved.

No part of this book may be reproduced, stored in a retrieval system or transmitted by any means, electronic, mechanical, photocopying, recording or otherwise without written permission from the publisher.

Based on the first eight weeks of mindfulness training at Pathway to Mindfulness.

Published by Pathway to Mindfulness, www.PathwayToMindfulness.com, info@PathwayToMindfulness.com

Cover Design by 100Covers.com
Interior Design by FormattedBooks.com

ISBN 978-1-7347220-0-0 (paperback)
ISBN 978-1-7347220-1-7 (ebook)

This book belongs to

_____

> "Don't judge each day by the harvest you reap, but by the seeds you plant."
> —ROBERT LOUIS STEVENSON

We want to thank our families and friends who give us much love and support.

We would like to thank each of our clients, who have educated us as they take their mindful journey. Each of you, in your own way, have encouraged and supported us through the years. Many have become dear friends and have made our lives fuller and more complete.

And we would like to thank each of you who bought this book, considering that perhaps a mindful life and meditation might be exactly what you need to thrive.

CONTENTS

Foreword — 11
Preface — 13
Introduction — 15
Conditions We Help — 21
How to Use this Book — 33
Setting Intentions — 37

Week 1 — 39
- Day 1: The Start of your Journey — 41
- Day 2: Getting Down to Basics — 45
- Day 3: Meditation Anchors — 49
- Day 4: Loving Kindness and Self-Compassion — 55
- Day 5: Meditation Posture — 59
- Day 6: Food for Thought — 65
- Day 7: One Week in the Books! — 71

Week 2 — 75
- Day 8: The Case for Journaling — 77
- Day 9: The Brain on Meditation — 83
- Day 10: The Brain Change — 87
- Day 11: Your Body on Stress — 91
- Day 12: Your Triangle Within — 97
- Day 13: The Pleasant and Not-So-Pleasant — 105
- Day 14: Stronger and Smarter — 109

Week 3 — 111
- Day 15: The Happy Quotient — 113
- Day 16: Happiness: Bring It On! — 117
- Day 17: Happy, Happy, Happy! — 121
- Day 18: Your Breath — 125
- Day 19: Your Breath as a Teacher — 131
- Day 20: Changing Behaviors — 135
- Day 21: A Week of Happy — 137

Week 4 — 139
- Day 22: P for Personality — 141
- Day 23: Dog Meets Polar Bear — 147
- Day 24: Is Anyone Listening? — 151
- Day 25: What About Them Goldfish! — 155
- Day 26: Stages of Communication — 159
- Day 27: By the Sea…. — 163
- Day 28: Halfway Mark — 167

Week 5 — 169
- Day 29: Hello Inner Critic — 171
- Day 30: Inner Critic: Part 2! — 175
- Day 31: Inner Critic: Part 3! — 179
- Day 32: Inner Critic: Part 4! — 183
- Day 33: Forgiving Yourself — 187
- Day 34: Body Scan — 191
- Day 35: Review — 199

Week 6 — 201
- Day 36: You are Not your Thoughts — 203
- Day 37: The Vagus Nerve — 207
- Day 38: Love of Self — 211
- Day 39: A Matter of Time — 215
- Day 40: Self-Worth — 219
- Day 41: Loving Kindness — 223
- Day 42: Week's Wrap-Up — 227

Week 7 — 231
- Day 43: Spoonsful of Love — 233
- Day 44: Make Stress your Friend — 239
- Day 45: Acceptance — 243
- Day 46: Impermanence — 247
- Day 47: Equanimity — 251
- Day 48: Gratitude — 257
- Day 49: Review — 261

Week 8 — 263
- Day 50: Authenticity — 265
- Day 51: Can you Judge? — 273
- Day 52: Awe and Wonder — 277
- Day 53: How to Say *"No"* — 283
- Day 54: Expectations — 289
- Day 55: Curiosity — 293
- Day 56: You Made It! — 297

Epilogue — *301*
Acknowledgments — *303*
Resources by Chapter — *305*
About the authors — *319*

FOREWORD

For about 50 years, I have had a voracious idea factory in my head, which drove my compulsion to find ways to improve my life. I've read hundreds of books and explored a lot of different ideas on my quest for self-improvement. All helped incrementally.

And then I found Bill Van Ollefen and Val Foster, owners of Pathway to Mindfulness, and my life changed.

I started looking at meditation about five years ago, but it made me uncomfortable; it was so far out of my comfort zone. Plus, I thought it was not a real solution for anything. But I was open to at least giving it a try, and spent the next year watching meditation videos and, of course, reading a few books. I was spinning my wheels, not fully grasping what this was supposed to do for me.

I did an Internet search, found Pathway to Mindfulness, and decided to give them a call. It was one of the best decisions of my life.

I have to say that the combination of meditation and mindfulness has turbocharged improvements in every area of my life. It's enabled me to become self-aware of what's actually going on in each moment in my life.

Each week, Bill, Val and I get together to meditate and talk about my mindful path.

I used to think it was a destination, a one-click-and-be-done solution, and now I realize my practice is a beautiful daily moment of peace. It allows me to see my life clearly and make decisions throughout my day that are better for myself and the people around me.

I guarantee a meditation practice is not easy. Nor should it be. One of my teachers in high school told me you will only get out of anything what you put into it.

I recommend putting everything you've got into meditation and mindful living so that you have peace on Earth not peace when you've expelled your last breath.

—Mike Shullman,
Partner at Russell Speeders Car Wash

PREFACE

At Pathway to Mindfulness we've developed a revolutionary approach to mindfulness, one that leads to sustainable change in our clients' lives and the lives of those around them.

We are insight mindfulness meditation teachers and mindfulness coaches, who spend our days leading others to the bounty that comes with living in the present moment, with full awareness and engagement.

The idea for this book has been percolating in our minds for a few years, but the motivating reasons why we felt the time was right is fourfold.

Reason No. 1:

We see overwhelming stress, frustration, hopelessness, and in many cases, malaise, in so many of our recent clients, and they certainly are not alone. These emotions that have overtaken so many lives can be helped with a mindfulness practice.

Mindfulness changes lives, in the most beneficial way possible. Since it is impossible for us to work with everyone, this book is an easy, step-by-step daily guide for you to immerse yourself in mindfulness and discover if this practice is something that could help your life journey. If so, you can use the book as the starting point to adjust the way you spend your life – physically and emotionally. And it comes at a most reasonable price!

Reason No. 2:

Our second reason is the word mindful, a word we adore while recognizing that it has become one of the most overused and misused words in today's vocabulary.

Misused: Everyone is told countless times a day to be mindful of this or that. What they really are being told is to *remember* to do something rather than to be *aware* of something, which is the essence of mindfulness.

Overused: The word is used so often it's become background noise, often ignored with a roll of the eye. That eye-roll is justified because it's impossible to be mindful of everything. Mindfulness comes from within; it is not something you can be told to do and then magically expect it to happen, although that would be lovely.

Reason No. 3:

Our clients have been suggesting we write a book for years because ours is a down-to-earth approach to mindfulness that adapts well to modern-day life.

Reason No. 4:

Our approach works – for hundreds of our clients and for us. We believe so much in the concept of mindfulness, we thought it was time to share our program with you. And if you begin to see it changes your life, we hope you will suggest to your loved ones that perhaps they give mindfulness a try.

INTRODUCTION

THERE'S A GOOD REASON WHY so many people have embraced mindfulness. They have:
- Learned to be present in the moment, living their best life;
- Discovered how to pay attention to what is going on around them;
- Become more grateful and appreciative of what they have;
- Realized how to feel more alive, not to mention good about themselves.

Will all these good things come your way at the end of 56 days?

As we tell all our clients – and now you – we make no guarantees, except one:

> *If you do the work, you will change your life and those patterns of behavior that need some improvement.*

We all have behaviors that could use a nudge, so you're in good company.

A new path

We firmly believe that if everyone embraced the true concept of mindfulness, the world would become more peaceful and loving.

We understand that this will never happen but will continue trying. This book is basically the 56-day program we have taught to hundreds of people, which now serves as your springboard for renewal. It's all about self-care and love, acceptance and allowing, and learning to live with presence in the present.

Consider this: More than half of your time is spent living in the past or future, ignoring what is happening right now. And this causes SWAP:
- Stress
- Worry
- Anxiety
- Pain (physical or emotional)

We like the acronym SWAP because that is what we teach our clients to do: SWAP out the negativity that unfortunately is all too prevalent in most of our lives and replace it with kindness, peace and tranquility.

We're not saying that living mindfully in the present moment is all about happiness. Life happens, and all too often it's just not good.

But when you deal with issues in the present — and pay attention to what is really going on — you can focus. You make better decisions. You might mindfully take a breath to calm yourself. And the more you do this, the more you learn to respond to challenges rather than react. And there lies the key to living a mindful life.

Is this easy? *No!* Everything in life worth achieving takes effort and dedication. Mindfulness is worth the effort of a daily commitment. There have been hundreds of studies supporting this fact, many of which we site in the *Resources by chapter* section in the back of the book.

Even seasoned mindfulness practitioners face challenges, but their response becomes different. The more mindfulness becomes a part of your life, the stronger your resilience to bounce back after a challenge. You'll become aware of the people, places or experiences in your life that often bring pain or adversity, and the greater your desire becomes to change.

The meditation factor

Mindfulness becomes your way of living only when you add meditation to your day. Some might disagree with us, but we firmly believe that without meditation, you cannot sustain mindfulness.

In the first day's lesson you will learn more about the meditation style we teach – for now we'll explain it as insight mindfulness meditation – and why we think it's the fastest way to develop, embrace and live a mindful life. Our program is based on meditation because:
- It changes brains and patterns of behavior;
- Our clients learn and practice valuable skills and tools that translate well into responding to difficult situations in life.

We're often asked if unguided meditation poses any dangers. It does:
- You will lose your judgment, hatred and your wants and desires, instead focusing on what you need.
- You will stop suffering – in body and mind. Your pain might still be present, but the suffering that is so hurtful will lessen.
- You can calm down your stress and tension.
- Your critical inner voice will become softer.
- Self-care and loving kindness will become part of your being, while selfishness takes a back seat.

OK, obviously none of the above pose any danger. We simply wanted to grab your attention!

Myth busting

It's also important to talk about some of the myths surrounding meditation, which make some people resist trying it out.

- **When meditating, you need long-flowing robes, beads or incense.** No, not required unless you love the look and smell. Nor will you learn mantras, chant or contort your body. You can wear whatever you want and be in any position that makes you comfortable.
- **Meditation and mindfulness are easy.** We wish that was so! Both take time, determination, stamina and discipline. It's a daily practice, which eventually becomes part of your routine, but that won't happen overnight.
- **I will fail at meditation**. Your meditation practice is a personal experience, and there are no right or wrong outcomes. In fact, the experience from one meditation to the next can be totally different. The only way you can fail at meditation is not to meditate.
- **Meditation is a religion**. Again, no. But if you study religions you will find that most have some sort of prayer or mantra that takes your mind off everyday thoughts.
- **Meditation will take away my edge.** This statement couldn't be further from reality. Meditation is not dropping out from life, but rather it's the fast track for focusing, facing reality, fully experiencing every aspect of life and being able to cope with what confronts you.

What about you?

Can mindfulness become yours? Yes! You simply need to embrace two concepts:

1. Understand that you can't buy mindfulness, that living a mindful life must come from within you.
2. Realize that no matter your age, occupation, religion, nationality, economic status – or any other term you might use to define yourself – you can bring mindfulness into your life.

But that means some work on your part.

Now ask yourself two questions honestly:

1. Are you living your best life?
2. Is there room for change?

We live by Henry Ford's philosophy: "Whether you think you can or think you can't – you're right."

If you believe in your ability to change you will succeed. You just must believe!

CONDITIONS WE HELP

MEDITATION, COMBINED WITH MINDFUL LIVING, is developing a cure-all reputation for many of the physical, mental and behavioral illnesses and woes of our modern world.

Let's look at some issues that have brought clients to our door, and see how mindfulness and meditation have a positive, healing, impact on their lives.

Addictions

Studies have shown that people who successfully complete a substance abuse treatment program – drug or alcohol – and then begin to study mindfulness meditation, are more effective in preventing relapses than those who never meditate. Mindfulness meditation helps people understand what drives cravings and how to deal with the discomfort those cravings cause.

Substance abuse significantly impacts the brain, and the associated behavioral changes related to the neurological changes are complex. Meditation physically changes the brain, developing new cortical tissue and neural pathways while reordering existing neural paths, helpful to the actual healing of the brain.

The mental challenges associated with addiction and sobriety are multifaceted. The incessant and destructive critical inner voice, coupled with the self-hatred and shame associated with an addict's actions, behaviors and destructive consequences are chronic problems. Urges, their root causes and the ability to control them, are a necessity for sober living. Mindfulness aids in the understanding of the whys of addiction, empowering mindfulness practitioners with tools to self-manage and change behaviors.

Mindful living and meditation affect real change. We include loving kindness, which helps recovering addicts find compassion and forgiveness for themselves, placing them firmly on track to discover self-love.

ADHD

The Centers for Disease Control and Prevention (CDC) estimates that Attention Deficit Hyperactivity Disorder (ADHD) affects 11 percent of children ages four to 11.

The Journal of the American Academy of Child and Adolescent Psychiatry and the CDC published research that shows an estimated two million U.S. children were diagnosed with ADHD between 2003 and 2012, and an additional one million more children, previously diagnosed, were taking medication for it. Most ADHD diagnosis occur before age six.

Then there are those diagnosed with ADHD as adults. According to the National Institute of Mental Health, 4.4 percent of the U.S. adult population is diagnosed with ADHD. Of course, this does not represent the adults who are never diagnosed.

Although ADHD drugs work, insightful mindfulness meditation can complement the drugs' effectiveness. Many of our clients are able to eventually reduce or even stop taking their medications *if* they continue to make meditation an important part of their lives.

A study at the National Therapies Research Unit at the Royal Hospital for Women in Sydney, Australia, showed significant improvements in ADHD symptoms in children who were taught to meditate. The children reported improved attention spans and less hyperactivity. Other encouraging side effects listed include:
- Improved relationships with their parents;
- Better sense of self-esteem;
- 50 percent of the children on medication either reduced or stopped their medication completely and continued to improve their symptoms through continued meditation.

Pathway to Mindfulness' program teaches you how to live in the moment with more focus and less distraction. Through meditation, you'll learn to step back and observe your thoughts and feelings instead of ruminating and judging them. Practitioners become less stressed due to reduced emotional reactivity; instead of reacting you learn to pause and respond.

Through meditation and an understanding of how the practice calms the brain, if you have ADHD you'll learn to slow your thinking, become more organized, and focus more clearly. During meditation, you learn to train your mind to notice thoughts, making no judgments about the thoughts, and then letting them drift away while focusing on your breath. This process does not happen overnight, but with practice, is achieved over time.

Lidia Zylowska, M.D., a psychiatrist, Diplomate of the American Board of Integrative Holistic Medicine, and a specialist in mindfulness-based approaches to mental health and adult ADHD, agrees with our approach. She is quoted in *Psychology Today* as saying: "Mindfulness is a state of mind that can strengthen by specific meditation practice; however, not all meditation training is mindfulness. The meditation training used to develop mindfulness skills is often called open awareness meditation or, in the Buddhist context, vipassana meditation." Vipassana is a cornerstone of our technique.

Anxiety

What is anxiety? At Pathway to Mindfulness, we recognize it as worrying thoughts that are difficult, if not impossible, to quiet or manage.

Humans think in the front of their brains, the cognitive part where thoughts and sensations come together. But deep in your brain is the amygdala, a major part of the emotional brain. Current research says you can only feel anxiety if your emotional brain overpowers your cognitive brain and forces its way into your consciousness. From the experts:

- Dr. Elizabeth Hoge, a psychiatrist at the Center for Anxiety and Traumatic Stress Disorders at Massachusetts General Hospital and assistant professor of psychiatry at Harvard Medical School, found mindfulness programs help reduce anxiety symptoms in people with generalized anxiety disorder that includes hard-to-control worries, sleep disorders and general irritability.
- Researchers at the University of Bergen, Norway, found that mindfulness-based therapies are as effective as Cognitive Behavioral Therapy – and are much less expensive – something we can attest to first-hand!
- Researchers from Johns Hopkins University in Baltimore, MD, found 47 studies that addressed anxiety issues – all meeting their strict criteria for well-designed studies – showing the positive effects of meditation on anxiety, depression and pain.
- Dr. Madhav Goyal, assistant professor at the Johns Hopkins University School of Medicine, led a study that was published in the Journal of the American Medical Association showing: "Meditation appeared to provide as much relief from some anxiety and depression symptoms as … antidepressants." The specific meditation practice that Goyal referred to is what we teach, present-moment and self-awareness without judgment. Johns Hopkins Medicine then went on to integrate a mindfulness program into their Psychiatry and Behavioral Sciences division.

How does mindfulness work in counteracting anxiety? When we discuss science on Day 10, we'll look at the brain in more detail and how it changes during meditation. For now, consider that during meditation the amygdala physically shrinks and its superhighway to the cognitive brain weakens, a physical brain change that limits the emotional brain's ability to take over.

During this course you'll learn focused attention, and how to pay attention to your breath. You will train your mind to focus on your breath, and when it wanders, to notice, acknowledge the thoughts that come, then disengage from them, returning to your focus point, your breath. You'll learn to look at sensations and thoughts as temporary, fleeting events.

The vipassana, or insight mindfulness meditation component, teaches you to suspend judgment or even evaluation of the thoughts, sensory input or emotions. You will learn to look at these events with curiosity rather than appraisal.

Instead of trying to make anxiety just go away, you'll learn to change your relationship with your thoughts and sensations as you discover how to disengage and disentangle from them. You'll be mindfully aware without judgment or evaluation.

Depression

We all feel sad or depressed at some point, a reaction to our losses, troubles or struggles; this is situational depression. But when, for two or more weeks:
- You feel intense sadness or helplessness;
- You think your life is worthless;
- Guilt overtakes your being;
- You can't focus and lose interest or pleasure in life;
- You suffer sleep or weight problems;
- You have suicidal thoughts….

…you may be clinically depressed, and you really need to seek medical treatment.

What part can meditation play?

Meditation helps you manage your mind – how you look at, and experience, your thoughts. A meditation practice teaches the mind to focus on the present, nonjudgmentally, and when you encounter unpleasant thoughts or emotions, simply be aware of them and let them go. You return to the breath without getting entangled with your thoughts. The practice isn't one of avoidance, rather a different way to experience your thoughts.

Depression also changes the brain itself, strengthening the connection between the medial prefrontal cortex – commonly called the "me" center – and the amygdala, your fight/flight/freeze center. The amygdala sends danger signals to the over-active me center, which ruminates and worries. Meditation quiets and shrinks the amygdala and reduces the signals to the medial prefrontal cortex, while returning it to its normal activity level.

Meditation is extremely valuable for situational depression. However, if you are in the throes of a major clinical depressive episode you should be under the care of a doctor; then you can start meditation, which is recognized as a significant deterrent in preventing future major episodes.

Insomnia

About 30 percent of adults have symptoms of insomnia, while about 10-to-15 percent of adults have chronic insomnia that is severe enough to cause daytime consequences – so says the National Sleep Foundation.

Before you reach for a pill to put you to sleep, consider learning how to meditate. It will help you get the sleep you need to lead a full, successful, calm life. You will learn to focus, as well as calm and reduce the thoughts and noise in your mind, let them go and return to your calming breath.

Your daily insightful mindfulness meditation carries into every part of your day, and at night, while you are lying in bed unable to sleep, you can use your meditation techniques to fall asleep, or return to sleep if you awaken in the middle of the night.

According to the Journal of Clinical Psychology, the breathing patterns you use during meditation are perfect for sleep.

Loneliness

Have you ever felt lonely? Most people have at some point in their life. The definition typically includes some variation of "being alone," although some feel lonely all the time, even while in the middle of a crowd.

Loneliness is a negative emotion, a state of mind that is not necessarily dependent upon the proximity of people. It is the *feeling* of being alone. It can be the quantity or the quality of our relationships that cause loneliness.

Lonely people typically feel sad, empty. They feel disassociated from others, often unwanted, with a driving desire to feel connected to other human beings. This state of loneliness makes it that much more difficult to form connections.

AARP says one-third of adults older than 45 feel lonely.

The consequences of loneliness?
- According to the National Academy of Sciences: "Loneliness and social isolation are among the most robust known risk factors for poor health and accelerated mortality."
- According to a study by researchers at the AARP Public Policy Institute and Stanford and Harvard universities, the impact of people living in social isolation add almost $7 billion annually to Medicare costs.

Neuroscientists are showing that the brain of a lonely person is different: extremely sensitive to social threats with heightened feelings of vulnerability.

A mindful life benefits the lonely in many ways:
- A meditation practice helps regulate emotional responses. The meditator's smaller amygdala, which is associated with

- over-reactions, dials down sensitivity to low-level danger signals from social threats.
- The practice of mindfulness includes nonjudgmental awareness of feelings and acceptance of situations.
- Loving kindness and compassion are part of this 56-day program, helping with self-esteem and self-worth. You can recognize you have feelings without going down a rabbit hole of emptiness.
- As you learn to tone down your critical inner voices, you are better able to develop deeper relationships with higher satisfaction levels.

When combined, all these changes help lonely people develop better connections with people they know, as well as more easily connect with new acquaintances. They become less likely to self-isolate.

Pain

While mindfulness and meditation do not make chronic pain disappear, it is becoming clearer how they help. Simply put, with Pathway to Mindfulness' program, you learn skills that transform your relationship with your pain.

The first, focused attention, is where you learn to pay attention to your breath. As thoughts or sensations arise, you acknowledge them, let them go and return to your breath. This alone allows you to look at sensations of pain and thoughts as temporary, fleeting events.

You'll also be learning vipassana, insight mindfulness meditation. This teaches you to suspend any judgment or even evaluation of thoughts, sensory input or emotions. You will learn to look at these events with curiosity rather than appraisal.

Combined, these techniques offer a way to disentangle from the experience of pain, both sensory and the mental impact. Think of it as awareness without the overlay of your thoughts.

Scientists have also learned that the brains of meditators respond differently to pain. During a pain episode there is decreased activity in regions involved in emotion, memory and appraisal, all part of the brain's pain perception.

Meditation's effect on pain is not a placebo. In a 2015 study by scientists at Wake Forest Baptist Medical Center using a two-pronged approach – pain ratings and brain imaging – it was proven that mindfulness meditation utilizes a different neural pathway, and with greater effectiveness than placebo.

The result? If you practice mindful meditation you will experience fewer limitations because of pain, the perceived severity of your pain reduces, and you will enjoy and participate in life even in the presence of pain. Your pain will still be there. It will be the suffering that changes, or in many cases, disappears.

PTSD

Post-Traumatic Stress Disorder and mindfulness cannot co-exist. That said, PTSD is a challenging and complex combination including state of mind, behaviors and neurological changes. We work with victims of domestic violence, sexual assault, veterans and others with PTSD and have had continuing, excellent results. But it can be a slow journey.

What is PTSD? In a tight definition it is a severe response to trauma. PTSD manifests itself in several prominent ways:
- The event is relived, over and over;
- Avoidance behavior for any reminder of the events is developed;
- People become emotionally numb, often with feelings of detachment;
- They become extremely reactive and have a sensitive startle response;
- Self-blame and guilt take over, resulting in low self-esteem and confidence;
- They experience high levels of anxiety, depression or both.

PTSD also affects the brain, including growth of the amygdala, which becomes overly sensitized to threats and danger, even perceiving it when it's nonexistent. When this occurs, it overrides and blocks the prefrontal cortex, the front areas of the brain responsible for rational thought, focus and other critical executive functions.

This is a lot to deal with, but mindfulness meditation is offering hope and help for those suffering with PTSD.

How does mindfulness heal PTSD? We describe mindfulness as living in the present, experiencing and observing without judgment and with loving kindness.

First and foremost, PTSD-sufferers learn about present-moment awareness, and how to live fully in the present, not the past where the trauma occurred.

Meditators practice focused attention, learning to pay attention to the breath. As thoughts or sensations come into the conscious mind, you learn to simply notice them, let them go, and return to your breath. You develop the ability to perceive sensations and thoughts as temporary.

The insight mindfulness component of our program teaches you to suspend judgment or even evaluation of thoughts, sensory input or emotions. You learn to look at them with curiosity rather than judgment and appraisal. This helps tone down and disempower the loud and incessant critical inner voice.

Part of mindfulness is acceptance and understanding of past events, not avoidance.

During the meditation practice there will be moments of thinking about the events. Yes, this is stressful, but the meditation did not cause the trauma. Utilizing mindfulness skills and techniques, you learn how to process and minimize the over-reactive behaviors and physical responses of PTSD.

On the neurological side, a meditation practice changes your brain, reorders existing neural networks and builds new neural pathways that can heal the brain. Meditation reduces the size of the amygdala, minimizes the frequency and severity of hyper-reactive events, while at the same time strengthening and increasing the activity in the prefrontal cortex and hippocampus, which adds clarity and perspective.

This is clearly a journey that takes time, but one that is on the forefront of PTSD treatment.

Stress

Simple stress plagues our society, young to old. The most basic parts of mindfulness meditation teach us to be present in the moment – to concentrate on one thing at a time – without thoughts of the past or the future intruding.

Learning to let go of these thoughts helps you worry less and accept things as they are without judgment or criticism. You are in control of your mind – your mind is not in control of you.

The brains of stressed individuals show distinct thickening and growth of the amygdala, which is responsible for triggering the stress reaction – our fight/flight/freeze center. While important to us and our survival, chronic stress with enlarged amygdala drives many of us to a level of chronic, hyperarousal.

You'll learn how meditation changes this reaction on Day 11, and believe us when we say, it alone is the reason we all need to meditate!

HOW TO USE THIS BOOK

Mindfulness isn't something you can purchase on Amazon Prime, have in two days, read overnight and say you understand what it's all about.

This book is your 56-day tour guide, with meditations, lessons, reflections, plus 56 ways to incorporate mindfulness into your daily life. All combined, these exercises will help you explore and challenge your mind and how you live your life, and understand and integrate the interactions of your thoughts, emotions and physical experiences. These activities are designed to make you think while developing a strong sense of curiosity about yourself and your world.

As long as you do the work!

Daily. Yes, it's that simple. Like any new skill, mindfulness takes practice to learn.

The Pathway to Mindfulness approach is much more forgiving than many other skills. Why? You simply can't fail at any of the prescribed exercises. You can't do it wrong. Mindfulness is experiential and everyone's journey is unique. Whatever your experience, if you accomplished the exercise, you can consider it is a success.

You see, it's the journey itself that changes you. Since the 1970s, researchers have been investigating, studying, testing and publishing thousands of studies detailing the impact and value of meditation and its ability to change our lives for the better – mentally, emotionally and physically.

That said, there actually is one single way to fail: Don't do the work. The only failed meditation/mindful exercise is the one you don't do.

You can't cram-study or speed read your way to mindfulness. Take the journey. Do the 56 Ways – one for every day. Speaking of days, this commitment is only for 56. Take one day at time, fully engaged and present in each activity.

Where to start?

1. Meditate daily.

Meditation is critically important to a mindful life. It's foundational, a cornerstone.

Over the course of the program you'll develop a personal sustainable 20-minute daily meditation practice. Scientists agree that 20 minutes daily is the optimal time period for the best results.

However, sitting for 20 minutes the first day isn't easy, so you'll start with fewer minutes and increase the duration as your skills develop. Meditation is what physically changes our brains and helps us train our minds to focus on what is important, to stop wandering about uncontrolled.

Good meditation/bad meditation? Again, there is only one bad meditation: The one you don't do.

2. Lessons

There will be daily lessons. Despite their simplicity, they take time to understand and implement. We have long-term clients who continue to re-explore the most basic concepts and lessons as they become more mindful, developing an ever-deepening understanding of the lesson, its importance and impact on them and their pursuit of a mindful life.

The daily lessons are short, fun and interesting. They are coupled with activities where there is a direct recognizable correlation between the lesson and activity. Do these activities with intention and complete focus, but most importantly, take the time to enjoy each. No matter how simple they may seem there is a purpose. Sometimes it will be about awareness of your thought process, sometimes emotions, sometimes your physical responses – and sometimes all three.

3. Reflections

As you'll soon discover, we practice and teach insight mindfulness. It is through these reflections, as well as the meditations, that you explore your essence of self.

You will explore your thoughts and behaviors, learning and understanding them. With this insight you can change how you think and how you act in a more skillful manner. You'll learn to live fully present and aware, fully experiencing your thoughts, emotions and physical self, in tune with the ecstasy, accepting the agony. You'll learn to live pleasant and not-so-pleasant events with equanimity, an evenness of your mind.

4. Journaling

An important component of the journey includes journaling. You will write daily during this program, about your meditations, lessons, activities and reflections. The journaling exercises will help you develop deeper understanding and imprint the concepts and lessons learned so they become integrated into your daily life.

We will talk more about journaling on Day 8, but in preparation, we urge you to buy a journal today, one you will enjoy using.

We have a journal that follows this course – *The Mindfulness **R** Journal* – which you can order online. If you like a less structured journal, you can buy one anywhere. What is most important is that you buy a journal that you will use.

SETTING INTENTIONS

Let's get started by identifying your purpose, vision, hopes, aspirations and intentions for the next 56 days.

1. What is my purpose for beginning my own pathway to mindfulness?
   _____
   _____
   _____

2. What do I hope to learn during these 56 days?
   _____
   _____
   _____

3. How can mindfulness change the way I live?
   _____
   _____
   _____

4. How do I want this change in me to benefit the people in my world?
   _____
   _____
   _____

5. What are my deepest hopes and aspirations?
_____
_____
_____

6. Now it's time for me to set my intention during these 56 days.
_____
_____
_____

Week 1

Your thought for the week:

> "The journey of a thousand miles begins with a single step."
> —Lao Tzu

Day 1

THE START OF YOUR JOURNEY

Welcome to the first day of your transformation. We are so excited for you, because we truly believe that the next 56 days will become the basis of your living a life fully engaged and aware of what is going on – not only within you, but all around you.

The first step in making any change is to commit, and we feel the best way to accomplish this is with a contract, one between us and you – although we'll never see it.

So, if this is for your eyes only, why do you need one? A contract outlines your responsibilities. We are only providing suggestions on how to adopt a mindful life.
- Contracts let you know exactly what you will be learning in the course.
- By keeping the contract in a safe place and rereading it once a week, you take responsibility for your involvement in the course.

Your contract

1. **Read every word we write.** You won't find superfluous words or thoughts in what we write. You will find concepts to reflect on and ways – 56 to be exact – to bring mindfulness into your daily life. We write tightly to keep you engaged and committed. And although you might find some thoughts repeated, there is a reason for this.
2. **Be 100 percent present.** When you pick up this book, set aside the usual distractions of the day and leave your to-do list someplace else. Silence your phone.
3. **Commit to 20 minutes of mindfulness daily.** In a few weeks, you will be meditating for 20 minutes, so your daily commitment might be a few minutes more, but we promise it will be time well spent.
4. **Action steps.** Read each day's thoughts and do the work.
5. **Believe.** Believing that you can change is the first step in change
6. **Journal.** Buy a journal and use it. (We can hear the groans, but we promise it can become your friend!) There is a companion to this book, *The Mindfulness R Journal*, online. Or, buy one that appeals to you.
7. **No fixing.** Mindfulness is a road map for discovering your inner teacher. We are not writing this book to fix anything you might want to fix. True healing comes from within. We simply offer the roadmap.
8. **Suspend judgment.** We all judge. Constantly. Ourselves and others. As you take this journey, instead of judging if something is silly, won't work, and can't possibly pertain to you, believe that perhaps it might change a little something within. Pathway to Mindfulness is all about no judging.
9. **Silence.** Silence is hard for many people. They live with constant background noise, at home, in the car, at work, at the gym. Silence is a rare gift in this busy world, affording you time to reflect without immediately filling in the space between with words. When you meditate, you do so in silence.
10. **Rediscover wonder.** Children wonder about everything, but as we age, wonder becomes something that happens every so often.

When you look at even the smallest things in life with wonder, your life opens and becomes so much more interesting.
11. **Possibilities await.** Consider your life an infinite pool of possibilities – or what one of our preteen clients calls a waterfall of possibilities. Life can get tough, you can get stuck, but if you understand that everything in life is impermanent, you learn to face your challenges in a more meaningful way.
12. **Do the work.** Do the daily lessons. Do the recommended amount of meditation daily. Do each one of the 56 ways. Vow to take responsibility and want to change your life. The more you practice and begin to bring mindfulness into your daily life, the quicker you change your patterns of behavior. You only get out of this what you put into it. **Remember, this is a daily exercise. Practice, practice, practice!**

Signed: _____ Date: _____

No. 1 of 56 Ways

Give someone you love or admire an unexpected hug. Or, simply hug yourself. Either way, pay attention to how you feel after you have completed the hug.

> **Meditation:** Today, simply take five deep breaths. Do this slowly and quietly. Feel the breath as it enters your nose, traveling down to your tummy. Follow the exhale as it leaves your body, either through your nose or mouth.

Day 2

GETTING DOWN TO BASICS

INSTEAD OF ROLLING UP YOUR sleeves, we suggest you roll them down, get as comfortable as possible and simply relax.

And believe!

Meditation is fundamental to bringing mindfulness into your daily life. We'll explain more about the science next week, but for now just believe – part of your contract – that what we are telling you is true. Meditation:
- Will help you change those patterns of behavior that need changing;
- Will help you lead a smarter, more focused and calmer life;
- Will teach you the importance of responding rather than reacting;
- Will teach you how to breathe.

Gaining insight

There are many types of meditation – Zen, guided, mantra, transcendental (TM), to name a few. We teach centuries' old vipassana meditation, which translates as insight mindfulness meditation. It is a gentle practice that builds awareness and can be practiced anywhere, because all you need is yourself. It is unguided, which for some is scary, and that is why we suggest you start with only a few minutes each day and work up.

We developed our program after years of study and teaching at Pathway to Mindfulness. We have incorporated a best-practices approach, maximizing the benefits to clients. This is a gentle, down-to-earth method with the intention of developing focus, ignoring distractions and promoting resilience under stress. We also incorporate loving-kindness meditation, which increases connections in the brain for empathy and positive feelings. Finally, we work on our reactive nature, finding and cultivating a more measured response.

Science tells us that meditating 20 minutes most days is what changes our patterns of behavior. We promise that if you believe and do the work, you will reach that 20 minutes by the end of these 56 days – if not weeks before. That is up to you.

What you need

- Yourself.
- A journal. We'll talk more about journaling on Day 6.
- A timer. Most of us have smartphones, and there are two free timers that we especially like because of their simplicity and ability to set the time you want to meditate – from one minute on up. We suggest you start your meditation with three bells and end your meditation with three bells, a function on both timers. Do not set the interval bells throughout your meditation – not needed and can easily distract or derail a meditation.
    - ✓ iPhone: Meditation Timer. Really, that's its name! It's a brown icon.
    - ✓ Android: Bodhi.

No. 2 of 56 Ways

When you brush your teeth, pay attention to the experience.
- Before you start, run your tongue over your teeth. What do your teeth feel like?
- As you floss, identify the teeth that are closer together; the ones that are farther apart.
- What does the toothpaste taste like?
- Can you feel your toothbrush as it cleans each tooth?
- Does your toothbrush feel different on some teeth?
- If you use a water flosser, how does each tooth feel as the water hits it?
- If you use mouthwash, feel it swishing through your teeth.
- When you are done, run your tongue around your teeth and feel how clean your teeth feel. Is there a difference?

> **Meditation:** Today you will sit quietly for two minutes simply breathing as you did yesterday. Eyes can be open or closed, whichever seems more comfortable to you. Breathe slowly. Calmly. Quietly. Focus on the breath as you inhale and do the same as you exhale.

Day 3

MEDITATION ANCHORS

We would never suggest you sit down, close your eyes, and do an unguided meditation for 20 minutes the first time you meditated. That is simply a recipe for failure. Today is all about the ways you ramp your meditation up to 20 minutes.

During meditation, when you notice your mind wandering, you will want to bring it back to your breath. Sounds easy but we promise it's not, since minds are programmed to think. When you sit in meditation, your thoughts will always be there – some days more than others – but there, nonetheless.

So, you will turn to one of three anchors – breath, visualization, counting – to refocus your attention on the breath. Why?
- When you realize your mind is wandering and use an anchor to return to your breath, it builds concentration.
- When you notice your thoughts are wandering and return to your breath, that is a moment of mindfulness not failure.
- When you learn to make no judgments about your thoughts, you begin to strengthen your self-compassion.

- When you notice where your mind wanders, you begin to develop insight into your thought patterns; this brings understanding into your life, exactly why we emphasize journaling.

As your meditations increase in length, you might use all three anchors during a meditation or only one. Again, meditation is experiential, all your own, to do it the way that works for you.

MEDITATION EXERCISES

You will now be doing a series of one-minute meditations exploring the concept of an anchor.

Anchor No. 1: Focus attention on your breathing.

Close your eyes and take a few deep breaths through your nose. Notice that your breath hits somewhere in your nostril. That point is different for everyone. Some notice the breath as it first hits their nostrils. For others, it's farther up their nostrils. The point where you first notice your breath is called your *breath point*, and it is a powerful tool to concentrate on during meditation.

You will also notice how your in-breath makes your chest rise and fall, or your tummy rise and fall, and how your exhale contracts your stomach and chest. You can follow your breath as you inhale and exhale.

Do not force your breath. Simply breathe as you always do, silently, calmly and slowly. This is not a race.

Set your meditation timer for one minute and concentrate on your breath.

Reflections: Pen/pencil time!

How did that go?

Were you conscious of your thoughts?

Were you able to concentrate on your breath?

When you noticed your mind had wandered, were you able to return to your breath?

Anchor No. 2: Visualization

You will now visualize something that brings peace and calmness to return to your breath.
- For some it is a happy place – beach, mountains, lake, a room in their home, church – anyplace where they feel calm.
- Colors can bring peace, although we don't prescribe to certain colors bringing everyone the same result. For some, black is peace, while others think orange, pink, blue…. So, pick a color that sings to you, knowing that one day it might be one color, another day a different one.
- Some people think of a loved one or special person that imparts calmness to their lives.

Set your meditation timer for one minute and concentrate on something visual.

Reflections: Pen/pencil time!

How did that go?
___
___
___

Were you conscious of your thoughts?
___
___
___

Were you able to concentrate on something visual?
___
___
___

When you noticed your mind had wandered, were you able to return to your breath by concentrating on something visual?
___
___
___

Anchor No. 3: Counting

Some people love to count during meditation; others, not so much. Again, each of these anchors are suggestions, to use or not to use. There are also no rules about how you count except one: this is not a race, so count slowly, possibly timed to your breath.

Some start at one and continue counting, others count backwards, and some count by twos, fives, tens, etc. It makes no difference because meditation is experiential – it's personal and all yours.

Set your meditation timer for one minute and count.

Reflections: Pen/pencil time!

How did that go?

Were you conscious of your thoughts?

Were you able to concentrate on counting?

When you noticed your mind had wandered, were you able to return to your breath by counting?

No. 3 of 56 Ways

Walk around your home and look at the pictures on your walls with a fresh eye, as if you're looking at them for the first time. Why did you hang them? Do you still like them?

All too often objects in our home become part of the background. We never really look at them.

Anything that no longer sings to you, take it down. Maybe you can find another spot for it. Or perhaps it's time to give it away or sell it.

> **Meditation:** The one-minute exercises were enough for today, although we invite you to practice any of the anchors to become familiar with each.

Day 4

LOVING KINDNESS AND SELF-COMPASSION

WE EMPHASIZE LOVING KINDNESS TO self and self-compassion because both are often ignored in our quest to do it all and take care of others.

We are not suggesting that you adopt a massive ego or become narcissistic. Instead, remember what everyone is told before a plane takes off: If you are traveling with small children, put your oxygen mask on first before you put on your child's. The message: Only in taking care of yourself can you take care of others.

Some philosophers and theologians say that before you can love anyone, you must love yourself. We find this a bit harsh and tweak that a bit: The more you love yourself the more you can show love to someone else.

What happens if you always put everyone else first and forget about yourself? You might feel exhausted, overwhelmed or resentful or even develop a martyr complex.

Enter self-care, which is not defined as weekly massages, facials or mani/pedis, although anything that makes you feel better is always lovely. We're talking about healing from within, where true healing takes place. For us, that begins with meditation.

To judge or not to judge

We judge. You judge. We all judge. In some cases, it is totally fine to judge. In most cases, we can learn to become less judgy.

Why is this important? Let's start with you. Think about your critical inner voice – which we will be talking about a lot during these 56 days. Founder of the Huffington Post, Arianna Huffington, calls hers "my obnoxious roommate" and the first time we heard that description we said, "exactly."

Unfortunately, your critical inner voice can't be evicted because it's ingrained in your being. It says horrid things at times, things we would never tell others.

So how do you evict that voice or at the very least make it less critical? During meditation you learn to notice your thoughts, make no judgments about them, and return to your breath. As your daily meditation practice strengthens, you become aware of what that critical inner voice is telling you and you learn to talk back, tell the voice that it does not speak the truth, and let it go.

The experience

Meditation is experiential. Your meditation is different from mine. And each of your meditations will be different. Isn't that exciting news?

Some like to judge their meditations as good or bad, but honestly, the only bad meditation is the one you don't do. You cannot fail at meditation, unless you don't meditate.

Some days, your mind will be all over the place, jumping from one thought to the next. Another day you might not recall any thoughts, it was so calm. Embrace each meditation and thank your mind for taking you wherever it took you that day.

No. 4 of 56 Ways

So how mindful are you right now, in this moment?

Who can say? But we do have a baseline survey that you will take three times during these 56 days. Today is the first of those days.

This is nothing to think deeply about. Read each question and answer with the first thing that pops into your mind. The scale goes from No. 1, almost always, to No. 6, almost never.

Again, use your gut here. You'll find the survey after your meditation instructions.

> **Meditation:** Yesterday you did three minutes of meditation, divided into one-minute segments. Today, you will meditate for three minutes straight. Breathe deeply and quietly. When your thoughts appear, simply notice them, make no judgment, and return to your breath using an anchor.

MINDFULNESS AWARENESS SURVEY

Instructions: Below is a collection of statements about everyday experiences. Using the scale, indicate how frequently or infrequently you currently have each experience. Today's answers, first column.

1	2	3	4	5	6
Almost Always	Very Frequently	Somewhat Frequently	Somewhat Infrequently	Very Infrequently	Almost Never

I could experience an emotion and not be conscious of it until later.			
I break or spill things because of carelessness.			
I find it difficult to stay focused on what's happening in the present.			
I tend to walk quickly to get where I'm going without paying attention to what I experience along the way.			
I tend not to notice feelings of physical tension or discomfort until they really grab my attention.			
I forget a person's name almost as soon as I've been told it.			
I run on automatic, without much awareness of what I'm doing.			
I rush through activities paying little mind to what I am doing.			
I am so focused on goals I lose touch with the steps I take to get there.			
I do jobs automatically, without awareness of what I'm doing.			
I listen to someone with one ear, doing something else at the same time.			
I drive on automatic pilot, wondering how I got someplace.			
I find myself preoccupied with the future or the past.			
I find myself doing things without paying attention.			
I snack without being aware that I'm eating.			

Day 5

MEDITATION POSTURE

We've all seen pictures of serene people, sitting cross legged on a cushion, fingers in a position called a mudra, angelically looking straight ahead with closed eyes.

Sure, you can sit like that if you find it comfortable, but we view meditation as an exercise of the mind that you can get just as much out of by sitting on a chair, which is what we teach our clients.

Some people like to lie down when they meditate – which is fine, except you might occasionally fall asleep – also fine because that means you need sleep. But if you find this happens frequently, try a different time to meditate or another position.

Others choose the astronaut pose: back and head on the floor, thighs at a 90-degree angle, and calves and feet resting on a chair or sofa. It's another very comfortable, easy-to-fall-asleep position.

There's another reason we favor the sitting position – you can do it anywhere: train, plane, car, bus; in a doctor's office; waiting for your kids to come out of school – an endless list.

How to sit

- Sit up straight, but not overly tight, imagining that a string is attached to the top of your head, pulling it up. If you slouch, your breathing can be labored. Sitting up straight, in what we call a respectful pose, opens your chest.
- Eyes can be closed, but if this bothers you, cast your eyes downward and try to concentrate on a spot within your line of vision or simply soften your gaze, not fixed on anything.
- Relax your body where tension accumulates most: shoulders, neck, jaw, eyes, mouth.
- Feet should be grounded on the floor.
- Hands are comfortably placed in your lap.

No. 5 of 56 Ways

Each morning and last thing at night say the words: "I love you (insert your name)." It's important to insert your name because you want this directed at you.

Many of our clients have a hard time saying "I love you" to themselves, especially one of our long-time clients, Eve, who came up with the brilliant idea of imagining her infant self and saying to her, "I love you baby Eve."

Within a few weeks she began picturing herself as a little girl, then a teen, a 20-something, a 30-year-old, and now she can tell herself twice a day that she loves herself in real time. These four little words have become such a part of her life that she tells herself many times during the day that she loves Eve.

Meditation

We teach unguided meditation, but today is different. We invite you to do this meditation by reading the words below or listening to it at www.

PathwayToMindfulness.com. It's under "Meditation" in the drop-down menu "Audio Meditations," titled semi-guided meditation.

It is the meditation we do with all our beginning clients. What makes it valuable is that we go through our senses and feelings and mention some things that might happen during an unguided meditation. There will be periods of silence in the meditation, which slowly moves you into an unguided meditative state. Let's begin.

What do you hear?

- Is it your own voice talking to you?
- Is it a sound in the room?
- Is it a sound outside?
- Whatever you hear, just notice the sound and return to your breath. Just breathe. Just simply be.

Breathe for a few moments of silence.

What do you see?

- Colors? Light shining through?
- Are you visualizing a person, place or experience that brings you peace?
- When your mind wanders and your thoughts come up, notice your thoughts, make no judgments about them, and use an anchor to return to your breath.
- Whatever you see, just notice the sensations and return to your breath. Just breathe. Just simply be.

Breathe for a few moments of silence.

What do you feel?

- Are you comfortable?
- Is there a part of your body that is tense or uncomfortable?
- Perhaps you could move a bit to make yourself more comfortable?
- Or imagine that you are sending your breath to this spot. Breathe in and breathe out. Do this a few times. Sometimes this simple act of sending your breath to a point of tension releases the uncomfortable feeling.
- Whatever you are feeling, just notice the sensations and return to your breath. Just breathe. Just simply be.

Breathe for a few moments of silence.

What do you feel?

- Do you feel a breeze?
- Are you warm?
- Are you cold?
- Can you feel your feet on the ground?
- Can you feel your buttocks pressing into the chair?
- Can you feel your clothes on your body?
- Whatever you are feeling, just notice the sensations and return to your breath. Just breathe. Just simply be.

Breathe for a few moments of silence.

What are you thinking?

- Are you listening to your inner voice?
- Are you thinking about tomorrow?
- Are you thinking about what you must do today?
- Are you thinking about what happened yesterday?
- Whatever you are thinking, just notice the thoughts, and return to the present moment. Return to your breath. Be here. Be now.

Breathe for a few moments of silence.

Tomorrow: You will need one raisin for the lesson. If you *really* dislike raisins, are allergic to them, or don't have one on hand, use another dried fruit, fruit, vegetable, cracker, candy – any food you can touch and chew.

Day 6

FOOD FOR THOUGHT

TODAY YOU'RE GOING TO DO a semi-guided, mindful-eating meditation, exploring a raisin with each of your senses, with full attention, fully present in the moment.

You'll also consider your thoughts as they arise, see if you have unleashed emotional feelings, and be aware of all your physiological responses during the exercise, recognizing the interactions among the body, mind and emotions.

You can do this meditation using the words that follow or you can visit our website, www.PathwaytoMindfulness.com. Click the "Meditation" header, drop-down menu "Audio Meditations," titled The Raisin.

As you read or listen to the meditation, do not make notes. Simply be present for the exercise, using the questions to help guide you. Don't rush it. Take a couple of minutes for each of the five senses. Let's begin.

Take a single raisin and place it in the palm of your open hand.

1. Look at it. What do you see?

- A raisin. OK that was easy, too easy. Look carefully, with your complete attention and focus. What do you see?
- What color is it? Is the color uniform? Do you see browns, reds, greys, white, blacks?
- Is the raisin shiny or dull? Perhaps both?
- What is the shape? Is it round, square, irregular? Explore its shape with your full attention.
- Does looking at the raisin elicit any thoughts, emotions or physical responses?
- With total focus and awareness, what do you see?

2. What do you feel?

- Can you feel the weight of the raisin in your hand?
- Is it hot? Cold?
- Use your fingers to explore it.
- Does it feel smooth? Can you feel the ridges?
- Is it wet, slippery or sticky?
- Does your touching the raisin elicit any thoughts, emotions or physical responses?
- With total focus and awareness, what do you feel?

3. What do you hear?

- Does a raisin have a voice? What a curious question.
- Place the raisin close to your ear and listen carefully. Anything?
- Give it a shake. Anything?
- Now roll the raisin between your fingertips.
- Do you hear it crackle and pop? Who knew a raisin had a voice?
- Does listening to the raisin elicit any thoughts, emotions or physical responses?
- With total focus and awareness, what do you hear?

4. What do you smell?

- Move the raisin close to your nose. Now close your eyes and with your full attention, smell the raisin.
- Move beyond the obvious raisin smell. What do you smell?
- Can you smell the sweetness?
- What's happening in your body as you smell the raisin? Are you salivating?
- Do you have any emotional responses? Happy or pleasant feelings, unhappy feelings, or neutral?
- Any thoughts? Memories?
- In addition to our mouths and salivary glands, our sense of smell is very tied to our minds, memories and emotions. Re-explore your thoughts, feelings and memories.
- With total focus and awareness, what do you smell?

5. What do you taste?

- Pop the raisin into your mouth but don't chew it just yet.
- Explore the raisin and how it feels in your mouth.
- Did you notice an increase in saliva?
- Now you can begin to chew it slowly; be aware of the burst of flavor, of the rush of saliva.
- Expand your thinking beyond, "it tastes like a raisin." How sweet is it?
- Is it a simple flavor or after careful exploration is it complex?
- Now liquified, swallow the raisin.
- Expand your attention to the physical sensations. Did you notice the feeling in your throat as you swallowed? Did you feel it hit your stomach?
- Is the saliva reducing? How has the taste changed as the sweetness dissipates? Can you taste or feel the tannins?
- Your sense of taste is also closely tied to your mind, memory and emotions. Re-explore your thoughts, feelings and memories.
- With total focus and awareness, what do you taste?

Reflections: Pen/pencil time!

Take a moment and jot down your observations about this experience.

What are your general thoughts about this exercise?

Were there any surprises?

With this attention and focus, was it a more intense experience than when you previously ate a raisin?

Did you experience any memories?

Any emotional response? Happy, pleasant, sad or….?

How did the raisin taste, same as always or….?

Think about this

If you watch a young child's initial experience with raisins or some other treat, they will mindfully explore the raisin the way we described in the exercise. Give them a handful and they'll select just one. They look carefully and then begin to touch and feel it.

Surprisingly, virtually all children listen to it before sniffing and eating it, slowly exploring and enjoying the raisin and the moment. They then take another and spend time with it.

Eventually they fall into a less mindful habit, grabbing a handful and popping it into their mouths.

We have done this experience with more than a thousand clients, and yet it remains a fun experience. The ties to memories are always interesting, especially when the clients close their eyes and smell the raisin, pleasantly remembering experiences or places long forgotten.

How frequently do you simply eat, mindlessly gobbling down your food or snack, barely noticing it?

No. 6 of 56 Ways

Do a mindful eating exercise with something you really like. Linger in each moment as you explore a favorite food or drink mindfully. The experience doesn't have to be super long – just enjoy it like never before. Try to incorporate this way of eating into your life, paying attention to every bite, although not exaggerating it as much as we just did in this exercise!

If you slow down your eating, paying attention to what is in your mouth and all the food on your plate, you'll enjoy it more. If you have some weight to lose, this helps.

Meditation: Today you will meditate for five minutes. When your thoughts appear – and they will – use an anchor (your breath, visualization, counting) to return to your breath.

Day 7

ONE WEEK IN THE BOOKS!

PAT YOURSELF ON THE BACK: You've completed a week of mindfulness training.

Hopefully, you have learned that meditation is the foundation on which mindfulness grows, and that you are enjoying your 5 minutes of silent reflection. We firmly believe that it is impossible to lead a truly mindful life without a strong meditation practice.

Throughout this week, you have been taking the time during the day to capture some mindful moments:
- You are really looking at the foods you eat and how you eat them.
- You have paid attention when you brushed your teeth.
- You are hopefully saying four little words to yourself each morning and night.

You have also learned a few things:
- About the type of meditation we teach – vipassana – and how it is the fastest way to change your patterns of behavior.
- You now know three anchors to use during meditation – breath, visualization, counting – to stop your thoughts and return to your breath.
- And you're meditating five minutes a day, fully understanding that there are no good or bad meditations; the only way you can fail is to not meditate.

But this is just the start!

Mindfulness defined

There are many definitions of mindfulness, but the one we use:

> *Mindfulness is living in the present, not thinking about the past or worrying about the future. It is living without judgment or criticism. It is simply being, responding to life rather than reacting.*

When you mindfully engage in life, you learn to breathe, explore with curiosity, nourish yourself and your loved ones, and ultimately thrive. Mindfulness frees you to enjoy life, happier, healthier and more peacefully. We are so committed to the last sentence, it is on our business card.

Through awareness you learn to tap into your powerful inner resources. You gain insight, transformation and healing – from within – which is true healing.

We would be lying if we said this is possible to accomplish 24/7. We don't live in monasteries. We live in the real world and face real-world problems daily.

But mindful people approach life differently. They learn to pick their battles. They surround themselves – as much as possible – with people that lift them up rather than tear them down. They learn that when facing a stressor to pause, breathe, and move on.

And if they find themselves reacting rather than responding, it makes them uncomfortable. Their new normal has taken over and they understand it's a much nicer place to be.

Reflections: Go back and re-read your contract. Commit again.

No. 7 of 56 Ways

After you greet the day by saying, "I love you (your name)," take five deep breaths. And when you tell yourself at day's end, "I love you (your name)," take five deep breaths.

> **Meditation:** We are holding at five minutes of meditation.

Week 2

Your thought for the week:

> *To be an expert means that you were once a beginner.*

Day 8

THE CASE FOR JOURNALING

To JOURNAL OR NOT TO journal? Definitely journal. We know: You despise it. Or you just might not have the time for it. We understand. And you're not alone.

But there really are some very good reasons why a journal can help you. We suggest at the end of each meditation, you write down some of the thoughts that came up during your meditation. We're not asking you to write paragraphs – unless you want to.

Keep it simple. Jot down the thoughts in just a few words. At the end of each week, look over what you journaled. Sometimes, you will wonder: "Where did that thought came from?" Other thoughts you'll recognize as big-life issues.

By jotting down your thoughts, it gives you a chance to think about them outside of meditation.

Some of the benefits of journaling:
- It brings self-awareness and insight; exactly what mindfulness is all about.

- It can bring clarity about those things that are bothering you.
- It can provide an answer to something that you have been thinking about, but the solution was elusive.
- It's a safe place for you to write about you.
- It helps you set intentions about the parts of your life you would like to change.

Take the time to find a journal that makes you feel good. We have created one – *The Mindfulness R Journal* – which follows this course and can be ordered online. If you would like a less structured journal, you can buy one anywhere.

At the end of this day's lesson you will find a meditation log that works until you buy your journal!

And while you're looking for a journal, find a pen or pencil that is comfortable to use. Some of our clients like a certain color ink, while others choose many different pens in different colors, and choose one daily that reflects their mood. This is your journal, so make it as personal and friendly as possible.

Reflections: Pen/pencil time!

Do you like to journal? Yes? No?

If yes, why?

_____
_____
_____

If no, why?

_____
_____
_____

Now close your eyes and think about all the good possibilities that can happen with journaling.

_____
_____
_____

Have you ever jotted down a thought or a quote, and days later read it again with greater insight? This is what happens when you journal – you gain greater insight into *you*!

No. 8 of 56 Ways

Breathe deeply at least four times throughout the day. Pause what you're doing and feel your breath as it enters your nose. Feel it in your breath point. Follow your breath as your chest and tummy rise on the in-breath and contract on the exhale.

Do one, two or three breaths each time you pause. Breathe slowly, deeply, quietly. We want you to get into the habit of taking breaths throughout your day.

> **Meditation:** Today you will mediate for six minutes. Following this page is a meditation log to get you in the habit of journaling. It can also serve as a template for how you will eventually journal in your book. The log is also at www.PathwayToMindfulness.com, Meditation tab, scroll down to worksheets, titled Meditation log.

The log asks two basic questions: Did you meditate? How long?

The third question asks about any thoughts that came up. And when you look at the space allotted for the answer, you will see that we are not suggesting you write a book.

The final question asks about any physical discomforts. Did you feel any of the spots that are tense in your body? The meditation you did on Day 5 suggests that you send your breath to any part of your body that is tense or in pain. This is simply a reminder to do this. As you begin to increase your meditation times, you might experience a numbing, which can be helped by sending your breath to that spot.

MEDITATION LOG

	Did you meditate?	How long?	Thoughts that came up?	Physical discomfort?
Day 1				
Meditation				
Day 2				
Meditation				
Day 3				
Meditation				
Day 4				
Meditation				
Day 5				
Meditation				
Day 6				
Meditation				
Day 7				
Meditation				

Day 9

THE BRAIN ON MEDITATION

MEDITATION SUPER CHARGES YOUR BRAIN, making you smarter, focused, more attentive, empathetic, less reactive and well, just nicer.

Are you too old to change? No! But it's important to keep in mind that our brains shrink as we age. Absent exercising our minds, learning and change become harder, our memories are not as sharp, critical thinking begins to dull, and we lack cognitive flexibility.

Neuroplasticity – the brain's ability to grow, change and reorganize – becomes more efficient through meditation. It's like setting your brain on fire, giving it a mega boost of growth that only gets better the more you meditate. More good news: You can shape the direction your brain changes by simply meditating and leading a mindful life.

How?

Each mindful moment – starting with your first meditation when you notice your mind is wandering and you bring it back to your breath

– begins to change your brain. That first moment of awareness starts laying down new neural synapses, reordering existing neural networks.

Now let's think of a behavior, for example, being judgmental, not that any of us are! Consider that your brain has neural highways that have developed and been reinforced over your life. If you decide you would like to be less judgmental, you must build a new neural highway, one that is more skillful or more acceptable to our intended pattern of behavior.

Guess what? Meditation builds those neural highways, and over time, new behaviors and thought patterns become your new normal.

No, it doesn't happen overnight. But gradually, as you begin to build your unguided meditation practice to 20 minutes a day – the time science says will change your patterns of behavior – you begin to transform. You can't help it. It just happens.

Your brain generally operates on what is called a Default Mode Network (DMN). When the DMN is active, your thoughts jump from one to another, without direction, and are often the cause of unhappiness or discontent. Studies have shown that mindfulness stills the DMN. You become more aware, more alive, less judgmental and reactive. It causes you to pause and respond to what is happening in your world, rather than react.

Our approach

The type of meditation matters, too. While all are good, different styles have very specific benefits. Some promote relaxation, others relieve depression or the effects of trauma, some improve focus, and others enhance compassion, kindness and happiness.

After years of study and teaching, Pathway to Mindfulness developed a meditation program incorporating a best-practices approach, maximizing all of the above benefits to our clients.

It is what we are sharing in this book, so it's yours now, too. This is a gentle, down-to-earth practice with the intention of:
- developing focus and self-awareness;
- ignoring distractions;
- and promoting resilience under stress.

We incorporate loving-kindness into the practice, which increases connections in the brain for empathy and positive feelings. Finally, we work on reactive natures, finding and cultivating a more measured response.

No. 9 of 56 Ways

When you get out of bed in the morning, go into the bathroom and splash some cold water on your face. Feel the sensations:
- Does this feel good?
- Would you like the water a little warmer?
- A tad colder?
- And how do you feel when you dry your face?
- Did this wake you up?
- Is this something you would like to incorporate into your morning routine?

> **Meditation:** Up your meditation to seven minutes. Complete the meditation log or journal.

Day 10

THE BRAIN CHANGE

Time to get technical and delve into how meditation changes your brain and affects how you act. We'll make a blanket statement that is backed up by thousands of research studies conducted over the past five decades:

Meditation strengthens virtually every part of your brain and its functions are enhanced.

This all translates into a better you. And best of all, the changes are permanent and integrate into your daily life.

We want to give you some talking points to explain to your loved ones and friends why you've decided to embrace a mindful life. The plus side to this is that even if you remember only one brain part that improves, everyone will think you are so very smart.

Close your fist, over your thumb, and drop your fist a bit. Say hello to your hand puppet. Your fist is your brain, your arm, the spinal cord.

Cortical tissue – or gray matter – covers the entire brain's surface. Meditation causes a measurable thickening everywhere here, so instead of the brain shrinking as you age, it grows.

Prefrontal cortex and frontal lobe are found behind your forehead; on your hand puppet, it's your knuckles. This is your brain's CEO, controlling executive functions and higher ordered thinking. This region is responsible for rational thought, helps regulate attention, improves your planning and organizational skills, and plays a part in your emotional self – all the stuff that makes your thinking better, smarter and clearer.

Anterior cingulate cortex is behind the prefrontal cortex (behind your knuckles), where your self-regulatory processes are housed. That gray matter increases here too, exactly what you need because it is the center for cognitive flexibility.

Insula: Open your fist and meet your insula – aka your thumb! The insula is where you understand your physical self, your emotional state, essentially who you are, your self-identity. The insula is associated with your instincts; your visceral feelings and responses; and basic emotions including anger, fear, disgust, happiness and sadness. How you experience pain is related to your insular health. A well-developed insula increases your compassion and empathy. Current research suggests this is where your present-moment awareness is housed. With a well-developed insula you become more in tune with yourself and others.

Posterior Cingulate (located under your thumb) is inside the brain and is exercised and grows during meditation. This region is important for your sense of self-relevance and your understanding of how things relate to you.

Temporo Parietal Junction (also under your thumb in your brain puppet) strengthens during meditation. This part of the brain is associated with your ability to develop perspective and is a center for empathy and compassion.

Hippocampus: Close your fist over your thumb again. On either side of the fist – below the thumb and pinky – you'll find your hippocampus, critical to memory and emotional regulation. Strengthening the hippocampus keeps you sharp and helps you learn and retain what you have – so important as you age.

Pons: Mid-brain you'll find the pons (just below the center of your palm on your hand puppet). Many of the neurotransmitters that help regulate brain activity are produced here. It's a bridge between many parts of the brain, a busy and important region that benefits greatly from meditation. The pons is a component in many critical functions such as sleep, processing sensory input and your physical functioning.

But more isn't always better!

Alarm central is the amygdala. The smaller the amygdala, the better able you are to respond rather than react. And you guessed it: meditation shrinks the amygdala.

Stress makes the amygdala grow, and here is where your fight/flight/freeze reaction originates. It's home base for anxiety, fear and stress. A smaller amygdala equals a reduction in all of these. You become less reactive and your higher-order brain functions work better. We'll explore the impact of an overdeveloped amygdala tomorrow.

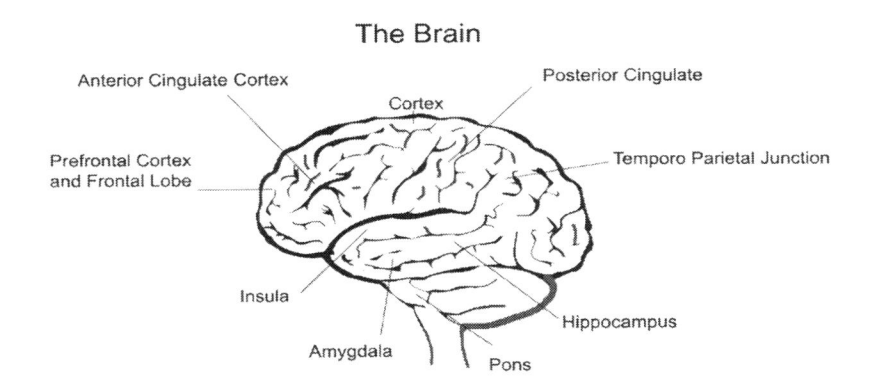

The Brain

No. 10 of 56 Ways

Some anxiety is good, bringing on a burst of energy. Embrace it! Maybe you can break your anxiety by doing something healthy for yourself – take a walk, clean your house, organize a closet, clean your desk, go to the gym.

> **Meditation:** Eight minutes today. Yikes! You can do it! And complete your log or write in your new journal.

Day 11

YOUR BODY ON STRESS

OUR BODIES HAVE A BUILT-IN fight/flight/freeze mechanism, developed ages ago when threats and stressors were external and typically life-threatening.

Picture this: You are happily eating lunch in the year 100 BC and out pops a sabretooth tiger looking for his mid-day meal. Your body reacts appropriately to this life-threatening event. Within minutes, you were either finishing your lunch or you were the lunch.

You survived, but what happened to your body internally? It starts with the brain's recognition of a stimulus. If the amygdala senses danger it immediately takes charge of the brain and activates the emergency safety protocols. This happens before the thinking part of the brain has time to process the situation; it effectively bars it from the process.

- The amygdala sends input to the adrenal glands, sending the body into a boost mode with a surge of adrenaline.
- A flood of cortisol is released, a hormone necessary to sustain the boost mode.
- Glucose is released into the brain and body for sharp thinking and to fuel the body.

- You breathe faster and your heart rate and blood pressure rise, oxygenating your blood.
- The blood from your gastrointestinal tract is rerouted to your muscles and digestion stops.
- Hello hyperarousal!
- The executive functions have been blocked, making it very hard to concentrate, think clearly or solve problems.

Bodies can only sustain this boost mode for about 15 minutes – long enough to react to the threat and hopefully survive.

You survived the sabretooth, but now the body needs to rest and recuperate. It typically takes two hours for the body to process the hormones and burn excess glucose, and for the circulatory system, breathing, heart rate and blood pressure to return to a normal state.

Back to today

Your body today responds to stressful situations the same as our ancestors.

While you still have immediate threats to your physical safety, most of your common stressors are thankfully not life-and-death issues. Consider what happens if you forget to set your alarm clock and are facing a terrifically busy day. This is not life threatening, but it can become a significant event.

Your body reacts to the late alarm as if a sabretooth tiger was in your room. The same chain of events previously described is put into place. Surely you can recognize this is a gross over-reaction to a failed alarm, but this is the brain's default danger response.

What happens next?

The late alarm sets the stress-reaction cycle into motion – and you are still in bed! Now late you need to rush, but recall you're not thinking clearly; it is now more difficult to function rationally. How much time elapses before the next stressful event? Maybe you spill a rushed cup of coffee on your white outfit, necessitating a change of clothing. Your kids won't get up. You get in the car and traffic is at a standstill or your train is late. Each of these stressors restart the sequence.

But wait! We said it takes about two hours for our bodies to normalize. In this evolving scenario that is your normal life, you've triggered numerous events without ever having fully recovered from the first.

Relating? For most of us in this busy world it's only the tip of the iceberg. We encounter events all day. Bad meetings, deadlines not met, angry clients, projects gone wrong, and family mini emergencies…fill in the blanks.

There's more. What about the good things in life that can bring on stress? Consider winning the lottery. Wonderful! But you will have the very same stress reaction. Or what if someone throws you a surprise party? Again lovely, but….

Do you typically get two hours between events for your body to calm and return to a normal state? Or did you spend virtually the whole day in a state of hyperarousal – without even noticing it because it is your normal. Tack on your own internally generated stressors, critical inner voices, a perfectionist mind railing over a compromised task, a lost sale, unmet expectations, dissatisfaction with life.…

…when do you ever rest?

You are not alone. Most of us live in a chronic state of hyperarousal. How does this chronic stressful life affect us? The constant state of hyperarousal and the hormones continually flooding the body are harmful. Scientists believe that a full 75 percent of our diseases are stress related and preventable!

The end game

Let's start with the "little" things. Insomnia and digestion problems become common. Headaches, backaches, general aches and pains become more frequent and worse. Anxiety and physical exhaustion start to take their toll on the mind and body.

And it only gets worse. If you have genetic predispositions to diseases such as hypertension, heart disease and diabetes, the risk of them manifesting themselves increases dramatically.

Chronic hyperarousal is also a problem for your mind. Your mind needs peace and some measure of pleasure, some way to deal with the stress. What happens? Often, maladaptive coping strategies develop, self-destructive activities that include over working, hyperactivity and all manner of addictions – drugs, alcohol, gambling, sex, shopping and over-eating.

How can you break this life of chronic hyperarousal?

Meditate! Live mindfully! You knew we were going to say that, but we speak the truth.

Meditation to the rescue

Most importantly, a meditator's amygdala shrinks. Remember this is alarm central, where the stress reaction originates, and reduced amygdala equals a quieter alarm. The super-speed highway between the amygdala and the frontal cortex – the center of your executive functions and rational thought – slows down.

A meditator's behavior in a stressful event is very different from someone who doesn't meditate. The stress reaction morphs into something more skillful, becoming a stress response. Meditators significantly develop present-moment awareness, and that allows them to respond appropriately to stressors.

When the alarm is late, your response will be an appropriate increase in your metabolism. You proceed appropriately, responding rather than reacting.

With a reduced number of full-stress reactions you eliminate the chronic hyperarousal. You also circumvent the maladaptive coping strategies. The result is that you become calmer, less anxious, less stressed, happier and healthier.

Reflections: Pen/pencil time!

Now it's time to think about your day. Each time a stressor comes into your life, write it down, together with the time it occurred.

Remember, the stressor doesn't have to be a huge event. It can be something like burning breakfast, watching the news, arguing with your kids to get ready, traffic, an uncomfortable conversation with anyone, a project at work – you get the idea. At the end of the day see how much time there was between your stressors.

Time: _____ Stressor_____

Time: _____ Stressor_____

Time: _____ Stressor_____

Time: _____ Stressor_____

Time: _____ Stressor_____

Time: _____ Stressor_____

Time: _____ Stressor_____

Time: _____ Stressor_____

Time: _____ Stressor_____

Time: _____ Stressor_____

Time: _____ Stressor_____

Time: _____ Stressor_____

Day 11 of 56 Ways

Sometime during the day, take a break and stare out a window. Look for something you've never seen before. Really look at it. Has it always been there? Or not? Look at the color, shape, texture – try to find as many descriptors as possible.

> **Meditation:** We're holding at eight minutes. And journal.

Day 12

YOUR TRIANGLE WITHIN

You have already started to think about the interactions between mind, body and emotions – memories, feelings and emotions that can be tied to your senses of smell or taste.

We'll take this concept a giant step further and examine what we call the Triangle of Self-Awareness. Simply put, you, your whole self, is composed of a triangle that includes your emotions, thoughts and physical sensations While each is distinct, they continuously impact and interact with each other.

If all is well in your life the triangle will look like this, quite normal and equal. Your life force is represented by the interior of the triangle, and is equally divided among your emotional, mental and physical self.

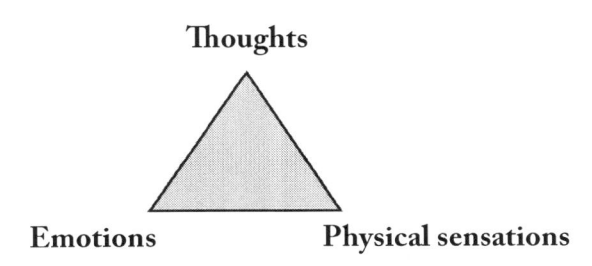

Thoughts

Emotions **Physical sensations**

Each point – emotions, thoughts, physical sensations – is in balance, with equal energy distributed among them. This is a good state, where you function and behave in your best manner.

Physical sensations

What happens if you have the flu? Or just a headache? More of your life force is taken by the physical sensations, which means that much of your energy is used or consumed by your body.

How much energy is left for emotional balance and clear thinking? Both will take a hit with less than optimal emotional regulation and subpar ability to think.

Emotions

When you experience emotional turmoil, your emotions are taking your energy. What happens to your thoughts and body? You lose your ability to think critically and clearly. Your body will suffer for it as well – you'll likely suffer aches and pains, lack of energy or a reduced immune system, making you susceptible to illnesses.

Thoughts

Thoughts racing? What happens to the triangle? You guessed it: In this case, your emotions and bodies are compromised.

Why is the Triangle of Self-Awareness important?

What makes this a valuable concept is the ability to use it as a daily self-analysis tool. When you understand the concept and develop a better awareness of your thoughts, emotions and physical sensations, you can recognize your weaknesses and vulnerabilities, compensating for them and functioning more effectively under adverse conditions.

We apologize in advance for the number of times we will bring up the Triangle of Self-Awareness going forward. Please believe us: It, like meditation, is critical for living a mindful life.

No. 12 of 56 Ways

For this exercise, think of times when your Triangle of Self-Awareness was impacted. Remember the effect on the rest of the triangle when this happened.

If you can't think of an example now, wait an hour or two! Something will surface or an event might send your triangle spinning.

Do the exercise once for each point of the triangle:

Emotional reaction: What was it and how did it affect your physical sensations and your thoughts?

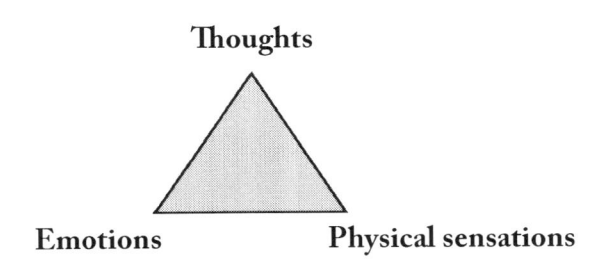

Thoughts

Emotions   **Physical sensations**

Physical sensations:
_____
_____
_____

Thoughts:
_____
_____
_____

Emotions:
_____
_____
_____

Thought reaction: What was it and how did it affect your physical sensations and your emotions?

```
            Thoughts
              /\
             /  \
            /    \
       Emotions  Physical sensations
```

Physical sensations:
_____
_____
_____

Thoughts:
_____
_____
_____

Emotions:
_____
_____
_____

Physical sensation: What was it and how did it affect your emotions and your thoughts?

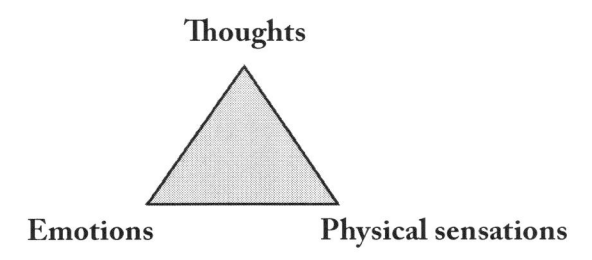

Thoughts

Emotions   **Physical sensations**

Physical sensations:
_____
_____
_____

Thoughts:
_____
_____
_____

Emotions:
_____
_____
_____

> **Meditation:** We're holding at eight minutes today. Use any or all three anchors to let your thoughts recede and return to your breath. And log!

But, there's more.

As we tell our clients, guided meditation is extra – magnificent *but* it should never replace unguided meditation. What follows is the script for the SAFE meditation, one we use in times of great pain – physical and emotional – when we need to relax and soften our bodies.

You can simply read through the meditation, or listen to it on our website, www.Pathwaytomindfulness.com, Meditation tab, scroll down to Audio meditations, titled SAFE.

The S in SAFE stands for soften, and many of our clients simply think of the word *soften* and it allows their body and mind to relax. This meditation has become a cornerstone of peace for many, and we hope you enjoy it.

SAFE Meditation

S is for SOFTEN
Breathe, soften the body.
Breathe, and as you exhale release all tension in the body. Soften.
Breathe. Soften. And now as you exhale soften your mind.
Breathe. Soften. Soften the body. Soften the mind.

A is for ALLOW…ACCEPT
What's happening? Recognize that right now, whatever is happening is not in your control.
No judgment. Allow, accept. It simply is. Breathe. Allow. Accept.
Let it be as it is. No resisting or clinging.
Whatever is happening – emotional or physical pain – allow and accept, without judgment. Just be.

F is for FEEL
What do you feel? What emotions are present?
No judgment. With great self-compassion and kindness: What do you feel? This is what it is to be human – to have feelings.
Show yourself love, compassion and kindness.

E is for EMPATHY

There are millions of people throughout the world who suffer, experiencing physical or mental pain, stress, anxiety.

Know that you are not alone. Show kindness to yourself and compassion to others.

Here lies your connection with all of humanity.

Day 13

THE PLEASANT AND NOT-SO-PLEASANT

Yesterday we started our conversation about the Triangle of Self-Awareness, honestly one of the most important concepts you will learn during these 56 days. It is something we discuss over and over with our clients because it brings awareness home.

As you begin to use the Triangle of Self-Awareness in stressful situations, you begin to understand how you *react* – and hopefully eventually *respond* – to life's events.

It makes no difference whether an event is lovely or horrid, it can, and will, set up a stress reaction in your body. Remember in Day 11 we talked about winning the lottery or being surprised with a party? Each is truly a wonderful event, especially if you have the tools to respond rather than react.

Life is also about embracing the bad, because without life's struggles, you wouldn't be able to appreciate the good. We need these contradictory opposites.

Enter mindfulness

When you embrace mindfulness, you begin to crowd out and temper your struggles by noticing the pleasant and what makes you happy. It can be as simple as smiling and wishing a stranger a great day – you get a boost from turning up those corners of your mouth! Some more good news: The more you're able to notice pleasant moments, the calmer and more peaceful your life becomes.

Reflections: Pen/pencil time!

Today you're going to search out one pleasant and one unpleasant event. Before you go to sleep tonight, answer the questions about each. Linger a little longer as you write about the pleasant event. Put yourself back in the situation and write about it in detail. Science tells us that reliving a pleasant event is just as good as experiencing it.

Pleasant event:

What was the event?

_____
_____
_____

Were you aware of pleasant feelings during the event?

_____
_____
_____

What were you physically feeling during the event?

_____
_____
_____

What emotions were you feeling?

What were your thoughts saying?

As you write about this event, how are you feeling right now?

Unpleasant event:

What was the event?

Were you aware of unpleasant feelings during the event?

What were you physically feeling during the event?

What emotions were you feeling?

What were your thoughts saying?
___
___
___

As you write about this event, how are you feeling right now?
___
___
___

No. 13 of 56 Ways

If tension or anxiety begin to take over, connect with your five senses. Notice what you are seeing, smelling, feeling, tasting, hearing. Poll your Triangle of Self-Awareness, focusing on thoughts, emotions, physical sensations.

> **Meditation:** Up it to nine minutes today. And journal.

Day 14

STRONGER AND SMARTER

We know we threw a lot of science at you this week, but we hope we were able to make it simple, translating it into something you can explain in laymen's terms.

You were reminded that many of us are stressed before we leave the house in the morning: One task after another, a timetable that finds us constantly running late, and to-do lists that never get totally done.

As you face each stressor, internally adrenaline, cortisol and glucose are being pumped throughout your body. You begin to breathe faster and go into a state of hyperarousal. Unfortunately, you never give yourself the time to recharge between stressors, so hyperarousal becomes your norm.

> *75 percent of us are stressed! 75 percent of our preventable illnesses are caused by stress!*

We talked about stress and made the case that meditation will help keep disease and maladaptive coping strategies at bay. We would love to see both of those 75 percent figures decrease drastically.

We also provided talking points about how meditation changes your brain for the better. Picture yourself telling your friends and family about the science, just proving that your brain is growing!

We discussed one of the cornerstones for building a mindful life, the Triangle of Self-Awareness that brings present-moment awareness of your thoughts, emotions and physical sensations to the forefront.

Reflections: Go back and re-read your contract. Commit again.

No. 14 of 56 Ways

Say something nice to a stranger today. If that makes you uncomfortable, simply smile. And then pay attention to how that simple act of kindness made your body feel – physically and emotionally. And what about your thoughts? Did it bring out your inner critic or were your thoughts telling you how terrific you are?

> **Meditation:** We're still holding at nine minutes today. And journal.

Week 3

Your thought for the week:

> There is only one person who
> can make you happy:
>
> **YOU!**

Day 15

THE HAPPY QUOTIENT

Two days ago, we asked you to look at a pleasant and an unpleasant event and write about each. Hopefully you did that and were able to see how each event manifested itself in your physical, mental and emotional being.

We also suggested you linger over the pleasant event a bit longer than the unpleasant one, because ultimately, we want you to begin noticing more happy events every day.

Why is this important? According to a Harris poll, only one in three people reported being happy. That's pitiful. We acknowledge that it's impossible to be happy 100 percent of the time, but the fact that only one in three identify as happy means that we have a lot of work to do.

The case for happiness

Why should we be happy? Simple. Happy people are:
- Healthier;
- Get sick less often;

- More likely to get married and have fulfilling marriages;
- Have more friends;
- Make more money;
- And are more productive at work.

Sounds pretty good to us.

Can you make yourself happy?

Yes and no. We like the philosophy that two New Canaan, CT, men, Matt Konspore and Mike Shullman, trademarked a few years ago: Choose to be happy.

Happiness is definitely a choice. Consider these two scenarios:

1. After telling yourself "I love you (and your name)" and taking five breaths when you wake up you then say: "Today will be a happy day, and throughout the day I will tell myself that I choose to be happy."
2. You wake up, forget to tell yourself "I love you," you never breathe, and as soon as you step out of bed you concentrate on your aches and long to-do list with a frown on your face. Throughout your day, you concentrate on the negative.

Is it possible that your day will be happier if you follow No. 1 or No. 2? Of course, it's No. 1. If you concentrate on the happy things that come your way throughout the day, your life will be so much more enjoyable. This is not just us saying this. Hard science backs these facts up, which can be found in our "Resources by chapter" section in the back of the book.

So, what's happy?

We're not talking about laugh-out-loud moments, although the more of those you have the better.

We're talking about little things that can bring a smile to your face.
- A smiling child.
- The sun.
- A cloudless day.
- Your favorite food.
- Fresh snow.
- Gentle waves.

Some of those things might be part of your daily life now – they just often go unnoticed.

So, notice! Look around you right now and notice five things that bring a smile to your face. Try this: The next time you are in a grocery store, head for the flowers, and really smell the scents. Honestly, this is the best way to transform a mundane shopping trip into a pleasant experience.

And smile more, even though at times it might be hard. We're not asking you to suppress your emotions. We are simply suggesting that you smile a bit more than usual. Winston Churchill knew what he was talking about when he said: "Your day will go the way the corners of your mouth turn."

Reflections: Pen/pencil time!

Ready to make yourself happy?

For the rest of the day, say quietly to yourself: "Today is a happy day and I vow to choose to be happy."

Before you go to bed tonight: Write down as many happy events that filled your day.

How did noticing these events make you feel?
_____
_____
_____

Did this exercise improve your day?

_____
_____
_____

Can you imagine how your day would have gone if you didn't look for happy events?

_____
_____
_____

No. 15 of 56 Ways

Are the corners of your mouth turning down? Say the long vowel Eeeeeeee out loud. Over and over. Until you start to laugh.

OK, we know this is ridiculous. But we promise it works.

When you say the long vowel Eeeeeeee, can you feel a tingle behind your ears? Some can; others can't. But this simple task of saying Eeeeeeee stimulates the adrenals and out comes those happy hormones. Isn't that lovely?

> **Meditation:** Time to increase the minutes to 10. Remember your anchors. And follow your breath as it bathes your body in calmness. Inhale peace. Exhale stress and tension. Inhale happy. Exhale unhappy. Inhale contentment. Exhale worries.

Day 16

HAPPINESS: BRING IT ON!

Are you ever your worst enemy? Without realizing it, you can stop your progress and choose negative thoughts/emotions over positive ones.

We've identified three myths about happiness that can challenge you from time to time. Since mindfulness is about awareness, if you recognize yourself giving into any of these myths, then you can start to make changes that will bring more delight into your daily life.

Myth No. 1: If you have all the necessities of life, you will be happy.

Your basic needs are food, clothing and shelter, so if you have enough of all three, then you should be happy. Really? Let's delve a bit deeper. Life is a series of ups and downs. When life is running along as smooth as glass, most of us understand that a bump is surely about to come along and slow us down.

That's life.

And because of this, your life is filled with a wide range of emotions, some of them happy, some not, and although food, clothing and shelter are needed for life, those alone cannot make you happy.

Myth No. 2: If you're not happy, there must be something wrong with you.

This was the philosophy that co-author Valerie's parents propagated starting at a young age. For her parents, no matter how you were feeling, if you put on a happy face that alone would make you immediately feel better. She grew up thinking that being unhappy was a bad thing.

It is impossible to be happy 24/7. Think about the pleasant-and-unpleasant-event exercise you did last week. When unpleasant events come your way, instead of masking them or making believe they are not affecting you, if you notice them, understand how they are affecting your Triangle of Self-Awareness – physical sensations, thoughts and emotions – you will be able to better deal with these events. Ignoring that they exist just brings its own set of problems.

The next time you feel sad, acknowledge it and know that there is nothing wrong with you. Begin to embrace your ups and downs.

Myth No. 3: Happiness is all about feeling good.

It's impossible for humans to feel good all the time since life is always in a state of flux. Think back to the pleasant event you documented. How long did that pleasant feeling stay with you before another emotion, thought or event took over?

Our definition of happiness is living a life filled with contentment, purpose and meaning, so whatever pleasant, unpleasant or neutral event is happening, you can breathe and accept the experience.

Reflections: Pen/pencil time!

Let's think about your needs, wants and haves. As you get deeper into mindfulness, the optimal state is when all three contain the same items – probably not the case today.

This is a great exercise to work through once a month, to see if you are beginning to make changes in your life.

What do you want?
_____
_____
_____

What do you need?
_____
_____
_____

What do you have?
_____
_____
_____

No. 16 of 56 Ways

Before bed, close your eyes and think of something that happened today that made you smile. That means that during the day today, you will have to look for something that makes you smile. When you relive the experience, poll your Triangle of Self-Awareness.

> **Meditation:** Let's hold at 10 minutes today. Journal, please!

Day 17

HAPPY, HAPPY, HAPPY!

Two days ago, we asked if you could make yourself happy. Today, we offer a dozen ways to tap into happiness to make that choice a little easier. Pick one a day and incorporate it into your life. Then repeat. And repeat again.

Hopefully you will embrace a few of these suggestions and bring them into your daily life. Forever! Why?

We want to crowd out as many of your unpleasant experiences as possible, replacing them with something that will make you feel happier, calmer, content – any of hundreds of good emotions.

1. Three good things

Nightly, journal about three things that went well that day. Add some detail about each, including how the event made you feel. Poll your Triangle of Self-Awareness.

2. Walk

Take a 20-minute walk and look around. Power walks are wonderful, but this is a different type of walk where you experience the sights, sounds and smells you encounter. If you see someone, smile and say hello. If you are walking for exercise and only have time for 20 minutes, consider taking a minute of that time to pay attention to what's going on around you: Turn off the music and mute your phone. If you find that minute enjoyable, you can start increasing it a bit each time you walk.

3. Happy activities for a day off

- Do something alone: read a book, take a walk, *meditate*!
- Do something with others: Grab a cup of coffee with a friend, exercise, go to a movie or museum, take a walking tour of a city or town near you.
- Do something meaningful: Help a neighbor in need, call a friend, volunteer at an organization or a cause that makes your heart happy.

4. A week of pictures

Put your smartphone to good use: Take pictures daily of something that is meaningful to you: family, friends, a place. Try to take at least 10 pictures by the end of the week, and then spend some time reflecting on the photos.
- What does the photo represent?
- Why is it meaningful?

5. Check in

Set reminders on your phone throughout the day to pause and take a breath. Breathe in peace. Breathe out stress.

6. Smile more

Practice this the next time you are grocery shopping: Smile and say "hi" to three people. See what happens. And don't forget to head for the flower department and smell the roses! Actually, smell all the flowers.

7. Be generous

Giving can lift your spirits. Tip the barista or the person handing over your take-out pizza. Give more to a charity this month. Be generous with your time. Help a stranger.

8. Forgive and let go

Holding on to your mistakes – or the mistakes of others – only brings stress. You learned that 75 percent of our preventable illnesses are caused by stress. It may take time to let go, but forgiveness is so freeing.

9. Find a purpose for being.

Daily, ask yourself the following questions:

1. What do I care about beyond myself?
2. What actions can I take today that align with this?
3. How will my actions affect my world?

10. Give some hugs.

Hugging another person can be soothing and healing. You can also hug yourself!

11. Look to others

Spend time with people who make you smile. Honestly, their joy rubs off on you. Studies show that we all are happiest when we are around those who are happy too.

12. Practice self-care.

Pay attention to how you take care of your body. After you eat and drink, see how your body feels. Get enough sleep. Breathe more. Move more.

No. 17 of 56 Ways

Easy: Take one of today's suggestions and do it.

> **Meditation:** We're upping it to 11 minutes today.

Day 18

YOUR BREATH

Meditation teaches us to settle down, to notice our thoughts, make no judgments about them, and to breathe.

Ah, the breath! At Pathway to Mindfulness, we take it *really* seriously.

The breath has the ability to heal and calm you down. And when you learn to take a simple breath, instead of reacting, you begin to bring calmness and peace into your life.

So instead of reacting you take a breath, and that pause gives you the ability to respond.

Let's face it: If you are running late, frantically dashing around the house is not going to make you on time. Take a breath. Concentrate on one task at a time. You might still be late, but you will likely be earlier than if you were zipping around.

Our systems are wired to be monotaskers, unless you are part of only 2.5 percent of people who can seemingly multitask. Interesting tidbit: That 2.5 percent are monotasking but shifting direction more quickly and efficiently than the norm. Our short-term memory can only store between five and nine items at one time.

Multitasking can also be dangerous, even deadly. Only three words are needed to convince you of this: Texting while driving.

Learn to take a breath. In fact, learn to take more breaths in a row, and pay attention to your breath. The more you practice this, the more you will begin to slow down and enjoy life more.

Three breaths

There are many different breath techniques available to us, but we especially like three – bellows, sequence and box breathing.

Bellows breath for rejuvenation: This is good for mental fatigue and to focus attention, especially at that point midafternoon when you might need a boost. It also works as a pick-me-up on long car trips. A few of these breaths work better – and faster – than a dose of caffeine. If you have high blood pressure, consult your doctor before you attempt this breath.

Instructions: Place the tip of your tongue behind your front teeth. Then bring it back to the ridge of hard tissue right behind your teeth, between your teeth and palate.

Breathe in and out rapidly through the nose, like a panting dog.

In-and-out breaths are rapid and equal.

Try this for five seconds.

Increase it for five more seconds, the second time, if this is comfortable for you.

If you are comfortable, increase it by five seconds more.

Today, don't do this for more than 20 seconds.

How are you feeling? The goal is to work up to one minute each time you need the bellows breath.

Sequence breathing for relaxation: If you are stressed, or suffering from insomnia, this is the breath to do. You can also use this as a tool during mediation to return to your breath when thoughts arise.

Instructions: Tongue placement is the same as for bellows breathing. Place the tip of your tongue behind your front teeth. Then bring it back to the ridge of hard tissue right behind your teeth, between your teeth and palate.

Start by breathing out. Now inhale through the nose, quietly, for a count of four.

Hold the breath for a count of seven.

Then breathe out nosily through the mouth, around the tongue, for a count of eight.

Do four breath cycles, which is one cycle of sequence breathing. Do four cycles of sequence breathing twice a day.

The goal is to do eight cycles of sequence breathing twice a day.

Box breathing for relaxation: Similar to sequence breathing and good for stress and insomnia. You can also use this as a tool during mediation to return to your breath when thoughts arise.

Instructions: Your tongue is relaxed in your mouth. You will be inhaling and exhaling through your nose. If this is uncomfortable for you, inhale and exhale through your mouth or inhale through your nose, exhale through your mouth.

Inhale to a count of four.

Hold for a count of four.

Exhale for a count of four.

Hold for a count of four.

Do four breath cycles, which is one cycle of box breathing. Do four cycles of box breathing twice a day. When you are comfortable with four cycles, bump it up to eight cycles.

The goal is to do eight cycles of box breathing twice a day.

Reflections: Pen/pencil time!

Bellows breath:

1. Did you like doing this breath? Yes? No?

2. How did it make you feel?

_____
_____
_____

3. What are some ways you could incorporate this breath into your life?

_____
_____
_____

Sequence breathing:

1. Did you like doing this breath? Yes? No?

2. How did it make you feel?

_____
_____
_____

3. What are some ways you could incorporate this breath into your life?
   _____
   _____
   _____

Box breathing:

1. Did you like doing this breath? Yes? No?

2. How did it make you feel?
   _____
   _____
   _____

3. What are some ways you could incorporate this breath into your life?
   _____
   _____
   _____

No. 18 of 56 Ways

When stopped at a light or caught in traffic, breathe deeply. Look around. You might be amazed by how much there is to see. If something really stirs your mind, poll your Triangle of Self-Awareness.

> **Meditation:** Meditate for 12 minutes today. And journal!

Day 19

YOUR BREATH AS A TEACHER

Unless you're sick, strenuously exercising or meditating, you probably never think about your breath. It is just there, doing what it does: *Keeping you alive!*

There are many lessons we can take from the breath during meditation.

1. **There is no drama about the breath.** It's just there. In and out. In and out. No big deal. Imagine your life with absolutely no drama....
2. **It teaches you to become aware of distractions.** During meditation, you learn that as you become aware of your thoughts, you use an anchor to return to your breath. Distraction of thoughts is inevitable, but as you practice meditation – returning over and over to your breath – you learn to notice, focus and build resilience.
3. **The breath teaches you to focus.** When you pay attention to your breath during meditation, you are focusing on your breath and what it does in your body. You focus on how it enters your nose and hits your breath point. You pay attention to how the inhale makes your chest and tummy expand, and then inflate on

the exhale. You learn to focus on your body as the breath travels through it.
4. **The breath makes you curious**. When you meditate and pay attention to the breath, you begin to see subtle changes in your patterns of breathing. You might identify a rhythm. If you are having a monkey-mind meditation – thoughts all over the place – you might make your breath louder to drown out your thoughts. You can use your breath in many interesting ways.
5. **The breath teaches you that you are not in full control of your life.** You don't control the way you breathe – the breath just breathes – like daily life where there are too many outside influences for you to be 100 percent in control of your life.
6. **The breath teaches you that there is beauty in silence**. Life today keeps you on high alert. When you regularly pay attention to your breath during meditation, you learn to embrace and be at peace with silence.

Reflections: Pen/pencil time!

Pick one of the breath's lessons and think about it during the day. Another day, choose another lesson and follow it through that day. The more you think about these life lessons from the breath, the more you will think about the breath.

At the end of the day, complete these questions:

What breath lesson am I picking today?
_____
_____
_____

When I noticed my breath, how did that make me feel?
_____
_____
_____

Did I choose a good lesson?
_____
_____
_____

What lesson will I pick next?
_____
_____
_____

No. 19 of 56 Ways

If you find yourself rushing today, stop, take a deep breath, and slow down. Poll your Triangle of Self-Awareness to see how this pause made your emotions, thoughts and body feel.

> **Meditation:** Continue with 12 minutes of meditation. Today, pay attention to your breath, as it enters your body. Notice your breath point. Notice the rising and falling of your chest and stomach. Notice how calm you feel when you tune into the rhythm of your breath. Just breathe. Just be.

Day 20

CHANGING BEHAVIORS

Do you have a behavior that you want to change, but have no idea how to go about doing that? It might be your temper. Or over-eating, smoking or drinking. How about texting while driving?

Life is stressful, and all too often you are controlled by your learned behaviors, that are now permanent habits. Habits are difficult to break. Unfortunately, you can't wave a magic wand and have them go away.

But there are three steps you can take to begin the process of change. It's also comforting to know that if it's a craving, it usually only takes three to five minutes for the craving to pass.

1. Be aware that you are doing something that you want to change. Awareness is so important in all aspects of your life.

2. Take out your journal – you did buy one, right? – and write down the habit. Then write down why you want to break the habit. Next, write about how your life will change for the better if you don't have this habit.

3. Perform the STOP meditation; words follow. Do it over and over. And then do it some more. Remember, if it's a craving, this urge will pass in fewer than five minutes, so performing several rounds of STOP can make it go away.

The problem with a habit is that we often do it without thinking. The more you perform STOP, the greater your chance of using it when you need it. It might even become a habit. How nice would that be?

You can simply read through the meditation, or listen to it on our website, www.Pathwaytomindfulness.com, Meditation tab, scroll down to Audio meditations, titled STOP.

S is for stop.

T is for take a breath.

O is for observe with curiosity what is happening. What are you doing? Why is this habit calling you? Poll your Triangle of Self-Awareness. What emotions are you feeling? What about your thoughts? How are you feeling physically? With curiosity, you might discover what is really going on and be able to stop the habit.

P is for practice responding rather than reacting, exactly what we learn to do in meditation.

No. 20 of 56 Ways

Throughout the day, relax the muscles in your face, especially around your jaw, neck and shoulders, where tension likes to hangout. Pay attention to what happens to your body as you relax.

> **Meditation:** We're holding at 12 minutes. And journal!

Day 21

A WEEK OF HAPPY

Three weeks of the Pathway to Mindfulness program are under your belt.

You are already meditating more than half of the time that science says will change your patterns of behaviors.

You learned a few ways to bring happy moments into your life, a list that as you become more mindful will begin to grow without effort on your part.

We also talked about the breath, why it is so important, and the lessons we can learn from it. You've hopefully incorporated some of the breath techniques into your daily life – box, sequence and bellows – so that when you need them, they will be there for you.

And you learned a meditation that we use all the time – STOP – that can break habits.

But there's more!

You are probably beginning to notice that a mindful life starts with practicing, and the most important thing you practice daily is meditation. We call it a practice, and implicit in that title is the fact that meditation is not a perfect. You practice it, but you don't aim for perfection. Your intention is to perform it daily.

We marry meditation with many mindful activities, easily incorporated into the rest of your life. You're doing them all – right? Remember, the more you practice mindfulness in your life, the sooner you will achieve a mindful way of living. The more you do, the greater your success.

It takes time. It is not something that comes in a box, is unwrapped, and becomes your way of life. But anything worth having is worth the effort it takes to learn it.

Reflections: Go back and re-read your contract. Commit again.

No. 21 of 56 Ways

Driving? Look at your hands. Are they tightly gripping the steering wheel? If so, take a breath, relax them, which will relax the total you. Want proof? Poll your Triangle of Self-Awareness.

> **Meditation:** As we leave this week, we are going to up meditation to 13 minutes. And journal! It really is an important part of this journey you are on.

Week 4

Your thought for the week:

Did you hear what I said or what you thought I was going to say?

Day 22

P FOR PERSONALITY

Effective communication is necessary in every aspect of our lives, but honestly, most of us fail miserably.

This problem is just getting worse as fewer people are talking to each other, instead texting or emailing to get their point across. We find this troubling, basically because inflections in voice or a person's demeanor are often important components in delivering a complete message. Neither are communicated well on electronics, no matter how many emogis you include in your message.

Answer honestly: Have you ever written a text or an email that has been misinterpreted? Probably. But the frightening part is that in many cases we have no idea how our message was received.

In addition to how you communicate, it's important to understand the four distinct types of personalities – passive, aggressive, passive-aggressive and assertive. What is so interesting is that you – and most everyone else – change personality types depending on the environment.

We introduce this concept now, because we firmly believe that knowing these personality traits will make you smarter while providing insight on how you react in different situations. This knowledge can also help you understand why you might not be feeling good about yourself after certain encounters.

Where do you fit?

Passive characteristics

- Compliant and submissive;
- Talks little;
- Puts themselves down;
- Praises others;
- Thinks they have no opinions worth sharing;
- Avoids eye contact;
- Tries to make body smaller;
- Hands are often fidgety;
- Gives in to others.

They are the people in meetings who never want to talk. If a meeting date is to be decided, even if they can't make it, they will never utter a word.

Their mindset: You're OK, I'm not!

Passives are rarely happy with themselves. Constantly giving in to others lowers self-esteem and confidence.

Aggressive characteristics

- Pushy and dominating;
- Talks a lot and over people, interruptive;
- Puts others down, sarcastic;
- Superior, always right;
- Believes their opinions are right and dismisses others;
- Looks right through you, not at you, and without emotion;

- Physically puff themselves up, bigger than life;
- Finger pointing and often in fists, clenched hands;
- Refuses to compromise.

These are the people that consistently try to take over meetings and talk over you. Should a meeting need to be scheduled, they insist on a time convenient for them.

Their mindset: I'm OK, you're not!

This personality is also not typically happy, often living a life of anger, resentment and inner turmoil.

Passive aggressive characteristics

This is a complex personality, simultaneously embodying and displaying opposite characteristics, expressing negative feelings subtly and indirectly, and separating what they say verses what they do.
- Stubborn and sullen;
- May speak or may give you the silent treatment;
- Puts others down using an insult in disguise, for example: "Good job. Almost as good as Mary's";
- Feels they are right, unappreciated and are resentful;
- The body doesn't show their inside anger but know it's there;
- Looks at you neutrally or possibly their head marginally cocked in defiance;
- Maintains normal to compliant physical presence;
- Limited hand movements;
- Defiant. May agree but not follow through or just refuse to decide; they procrastinate and display avoidance behaviors.

These are the people in meetings agreeing to a project then never doing their part or procrastinating in defiance. Should a meeting need to be scheduled they'll agree, then not show if it's not scheduled when they wanted.

Their mindset: I'm not okay, but better than you!

This is another unhappy personality, always feeling undervalued unappreciated, harboring anger and resentment.

Assertive characteristics

- Actions/expressions fit with words spoken;
- Speaks with clear messages;
- Respectful of self and others;
- Can see multiple points of view;
- Warm, welcoming, friendly, makes eye contact;
- Respects other opinions;
- Normal body posture and hand movements;

In the same business meeting, they are open and interactive, effectively communicating their ideas. When scheduling a meeting they will look at their own schedule and suggest alternatives if they're not available, and ultimately work for a mutually agreeable time.

Their mindset: I'm OK, you're OK!

Believes all are equal and deserving of respect.

Assertive personality types are the happiest. Confident and with a healthy sense of self, they exhibit good interpersonal skills and maintain healthy relationships.

Where did you see yourself?

While we all have a dominant personality style, we are an infinite pool of possibilities and our personality may be circumstantial.

How aggressive will you be with a boss? Do you default to a passive mode or can you be assertive?

Can you tame your aggressive side when dealing with a problem employee? How about a child who has misbehaved?

Why is this important?

Insight into your own and others' personalities helps you understand the complex dynamics of communications and gives tips for dealing with others.

Easiest example: An aggressive who is shouting at you doesn't value your opinion and doesn't care about what you think. Argue? Why would you? Let them shout themselves out; don't feed their anger. Without an active participant they run out of steam.

Interacting with a passive? Delve a little deeper, work a bit harder to understand their real position.

Passive Aggressive. Be very alert and be wary of agreement and commitment. Watch your back.

Reflections: Pen/pencil time!

Think about a difficult conversation you've recently had. What is it?
_____
_____
_____

Try to determine the other person's personality type. What is it?
_____
_____
_____

What personality characteristics were you exhibiting during the conversation?
_____
_____
_____

Was the outcome what you desired?
___
___
___

Was the outcome what the other person desired?
___
___
___

What could you have done for more effective communications and interactions?
___
___
___

No. 22 of 56 Ways

Call a friend you haven't spoken to in a while and share something about them you like or admire. Once the call is over, poll your Triangle of Self-Awareness.

> **Meditation:** We're holding at 13 minutes of meditation. Journal. Are you discovering any recurring thoughts?

Day 23

DOG MEETS POLAR BEAR

THERE ARE MANY VERSIONS OF the story we are about to relate, but we're sticking to this one – because we love it – although the eventual outcome is what is open to debate.

The story serves as a terrific visual for our clients to picture when they are trying to be assertive while dealing with an aggressive.

So here goes:

Way up in northern Canada is a town where the polar bears come out of hibernation, and where the means of transportation during the winter is dogsled. That means there are lots of huskies around, and unfortunately many of these dogs become dinner for the hungry polar bears.

One day a man looked out his window to see a polar bear approaching his husky, we'll call him Churchill. But instead of growling and barking at the polar bear – which makes polar bears angry and even hungrier – Churchill got down on his haunches with his tail wagging faster than the wind was blowing.

The hungry polar bear looked, and instead of acting aggressively, he began to play with Churchill. They had a great old time, rolling around the snow, hugging each other, cuddling – just what four-legged friends do.

The insula – you learned about that on Day 10 – of these two animals connected. And instead of acting aggressively toward each other, they played.

The lesson?

The next time you meet a polar-bear personality – aggressive, mean, argumentative – instead of arguing back or trying to get him or her to change, go silent. Yes, this can be uncomfortable, and it might not be the way you would normally react, but we promise it can be effective.

Take a deep breath instead of saying anything. Not one word! No one said this is easy.

But guess what happens when you go silent? Aggressive personalities will eventually run out of steam. They can't talk or scream forever. Ultimately, they calm down or walk away. If they stay in place, when they are calm you can start talking, with composure, intention and purpose. And lots of deep breaths.

This is what leads to better communication.

Silence

Silence scares many of us. It makes us uncomfortable.

With meditation, you are silent. The more you meditate the more silence becomes your friend. Wouldn't this be wonderful if it happened overnight? It doesn't, although the more consistently you meditate, the faster you get to embrace silence for what it is: Peaceful!

Soon, you will begin to crave silence. Many who once immediately turned on the TV or music when they got home, find this is no longer the case.

No. 23 of 56 Ways

The next time you are in your car alone, do not turn on the radio. You might have to *gently* smack your hand, but that's OK – you're making a point! Listen to the sounds around you. Pay attention to the sights you're passing. If this is difficult, start with 5 minutes and work up. Did the silence make you uncomfortable? To discover how, poll your Triangle of Self-Awareness – thoughts, emotions, body.

> **Meditation:** Enjoy your 13 minutes of meditation. Enjoy the silence. Journal after the meditation.

Day 24

IS ANYONE LISTENING?

Have you ever sat with a group of people, and you say something, and the next person says exactly what you said – just in different words. And then a third person does the same thing, and on and on.

No one is listening to a word the other person is saying. They are simply paying attention to their thoughts – and when they get a chance, regurgitate those thoughts outward.

And then there are those people who are constantly interrupting you. If you do it, know you are not alone.

Consider these sentences:

1. Did you hear what I said or what you thought I was going to say?

2. Do you listen with the intent to fix?

3. Do you interrupt?

We probably all do a little – or a lot – of all of these. Some ways to change:

- Let people *talk and finish* their thoughts.
- *And listen.* Really listen. Make eye contact, which keeps you engaged.
- *Don't interrupt.* Don't interject your own feelings into the conversation. Don't make judgments.
- Don't listen with the intent to tell somebody what to do or how to *fix* the situation. Just listen.

Meet the diad

Diads are amazing tools to develop sharper communication skills. Some of our clients jump at the chance to diad, while others would rather do anything else, but that never stops us from continuing with one.

Your immediate reaction the first time you are part of a diad is that it's a speaking exercise. Actually, it's more a listening exercise.

It works like this:

- Find a partner and a timer.
- One person speaks for two minutes about anything. Two minutes sounds like a short period of time, but often, not so short! The person who is talking can switch topics as many times as s/he wants until the two minutes are up.
- The other person just listens. No talking!
- When it's the second person's turn to speak for two minutes, s/he can either address what the first person talked about or ignore those thoughts and talk about whatever is on his or her mind.
- This exercise is usually done in pairs but can easily be done in a group if you have some time. It's a great exercise to do with your family at dinner. It might even get your teens to start talking, although we are not promising that outcome.

Basic ground rules:

- Let people talk and finish their thoughts.
- Listen. Listen deeply to learn.
- Don't interrupt. No interjecting your thoughts into the conversation. And no judgment.
- Don't listen with the intent to tell somebody what to do or how to fix the situation.

Client's experience

When Sally took our eight-week introductory lesson, she was walking her dog daily with a friend for 20 minutes.

On the walk that Sally took after her first diad with us, her friend started talking about something in her life that was greatly affecting her. Sally was about to say something to her friend, but remembering the lesson, decided to let her friend talk. And talk she did – for the whole 20 minutes. Sally didn't utter a word.

The next week Sally told us about what had happened on her walk, and she was amazed by what transpired.

- Although normally she would have peppered this conversation with lots of questions, by the end of the walk, every question Sally would have asked was answered.
- Her friend told Sally how appreciative she was to be able to talk with no interruptions. She thanked Sally for listening and for not trying to fix anything.
- Sally felt great about the experience because she realized she had really helped her friend work through a problem, without giving her any advice at all.

No. 24 of 56 Ways

For the remainder of the week, when someone is talking to you or you are in a meeting, really listen to what other people are saying. Make eye contact. Sit up straight. Be alert. Engaged. This all combined takes concentration but fosters good listening. At the end of the conversation or meeting, poll your Triangle of Self-Awareness to see how your body responded to this exercise.

> **Meditation:** Increase your time by one minute, to 14 minutes today. When your mind wanders, use an anchor to return to your breath. Don't forget to journal.

Day 25

WHAT ABOUT THEM GOLDFISH!

A 2015 MICROSOFT STUDY FOUND the attention span of humans is eight seconds. But let's put this into perspective: the attention span of goldfish is nine seconds.

We are in so much trouble!

We have another factoid we can't resist throwing in: Our minds on average wander 53-60 percent of the time. That means that in a typical eight-hour workday, more than four hours are spent not focusing on the task at hand.

People underestimate the importance of daily communications, especially in this era of texts, Snapchat, Instagram, Twitter, where short and fast are always best. There are a million opportunities for someone to misinterpret the message you are trying to deliver when it comes on social media.

Enter Mindfulness

Mindfulness teaches you to live in the present moment, paying attention to what others are saying, and the words you are using.

Consider this: When your mind is too busy and chaotic thinking about the numerous facets of your life, it's often hard to say the right things or listen to what another is saying. And when you listen, you will find the right words to respond, with thoughts that are your own and not someone else's ideas. You are calm, focused and in control.

You possess these qualities. You merely need to tap into your inner reserves.

Practice

The next time you have a conversation with someone:

1. Make eye contact.
2. Focus on their words.
3. If you find your mind wandering, take a few deep breaths and bring your thoughts back to the person talking.
4. Sit or stand tall. Good posture improves your focus.
5. Do not interrupt. If you have a question, wait for a break in the conversation. If you need to clarify a point, put up your finger and say, with a smile on your face: "Would you please repeat that thought. I am not sure I understand."

Difficult conversations

We all have them, and if we pay attention to what is really going on, we can learn from them so hopefully our next challenging conversation might be more productive.

Reflectionss: Pen/pencil time!

Let's dissect a conversation:

1. **Describe the situation.** Who was present and what was the subject?
   _____
   _____
   _____

2. **Identify the issue.** How did it come about?
   _____
   _____
   _____

3. **Your outcomes:**
   a. What did you want to get out of the conversation?
      _____
      _____
      _____

   b. What did you really get?
      _____
      _____
      _____

4. **Their outcomes:**
   a. Do you know what the other person(s) wanted to get out of the conversation?
      _____
      _____
      _____

   b. What did the other person(s) actually get?
      _____
      _____
      _____

5. **How did you feel during the conversation?** Poll your Triangle of Self-Awareness: thoughts, emotions, physical sensations.

   _____
   _____
   _____

6. **How do you feel now writing about the conversation?** Poll your Triangle of Self-Awareness: thoughts, emotions, physical sensations.

   _____
   _____
   _____

7. **Thinking ahead:** How would you have handled the conversation differently?

   _____
   _____
   _____

No. 25 of 56 Ways

Really listen to what someone is telling you today. If you are alone today, turn on the news and listen intently to one segment of news. Of course, we are going to tell you to poll your Triangle of Self-Awareness, and we are sorry for being repetitive, but this is so important to building a mindful life. We promise eventually it will become second nature to you, at least most days!

> **Meditation:** 14 minutes of meditation today. When your thoughts come up, notice your thoughts, make no judgments, and use an anchor to return to your breath. Journal!

Day 26

STAGES OF COMMUNICATION

There are four stages of communication:

1. What you intend to say.
2. What you wind up saying.
3. What the other person hears.
4. What the other person thinks you mean.

Interpretation is key here. We all think differently and in any given situation, there might be many ways to describe what really went on. This alone is one of the reasons many of us make assumptions about situations or what was said or jump to the wrong conclusions.

When you understand the four communication stages, we promise your conversations will become grounded in fact, not assumptions.

What you intend to say: Before you even open your mouth, you plan the words that you want to say.

What you wind up saying: In way too many cases, what we planned on saying is not what comes out of our mouths. Don't feel badly – most of us do this.

What the other person hears: This is out of your control, totally contingent on whether the person is paying attention to what you are saying.

What the other person thinks you mean: This is where jumping to wrong conclusions or making assumptions comes into play.

This theory in use

In any conversation, determine the stage you are in.

Are you speaking? If so, are you getting your point across? (The latter is hard to determine but if the person you are speaking to is engaged and asking good questions, you probably are.)

If you are listening, are you interpreting what the other person is saying? Are you being selective about what you are hearing? Are you forming conclusions or deciding what to do or say next before the person stops speaking?

At the end of the conversation

- Did you make any assumptions? If so, why? Past history? Or current?
- Do you often make assumptions?
- Do you make assumptions too quickly?
- Do you base your conclusions on facts?

No. 26 of 56 Ways

When someone asks you how you are today, say "terrific." And watch the reaction. Surprise? Delight? Questioning? This really can be a fun exercise. And – you guessed it – poll your Triangle of Self-Awareness. How did saying "terrific" out loud make you feel? This is especially helpful on a day you are feeling anything but terrific.

Meditation: Still 14 minutes. Don't forget to journal.

Day 27

BY THE SEA....

TODAY WE ARE GOING TO talk about two of our favorite meditations, both are on our website, www.PathwaytoMindfulness, and so easy to visualize. Once you do both a few times they are yours to use whenever needed in your unguided meditation or throughout the day.

Both are perfect for calming anxiety; a discomfort, either physical or emotional; or to ward off a craving. Both deal with the ocean, which many of us find very comforting and soothing, as we watch the waves break and then gently roll onto shore.

We introduce them here because communications can often bring on anxiety or discomfort. And if you are prone to a craving, a difficult conversation could lead to an eating binge or a few too-many glasses of wine.

Hey, life happens. We are just offering some mindful ways to bring peace into yours!

Find both meditations (the first is called The sea; the second, The wave) on our website, www.PathwayToMindfulness.com, Meditation tab, scroll down to Audio meditations.

The sea

Life is unpredictable. And can often become very stressful or hard. Right now, in this minute, we want to keep our emotions and feelings in check by thinking about the sea.

Visualize yourself at the beach, sitting on the warm sand. A refreshing breeze is caressing your body. You feel safe. Secure. As you watch the waves drift in and out, imagine that each wave is like your breath, rising from deep within you, and then releasing and returning to the sea.

Look at the surface of the ocean. Consider that it is much like your life – rough, choppy, with waves of uncertainty springing up at any time. Like the shifting waves, breathe in the moments of your life that are challenging and upsetting. You have faced these moments before. You have the strength and stability to weather any storm. Breathe out your fears and any doubts you might have. What will be will be. Breathe in life's challenges. Breathe out any fears or doubts you have.

Now let's consider what is happening below the waves, underneath the surface. It is a calm, serene, quiet, contemplative place to be. Schools of fish are swimming to and fro. Sea plants are swaying to a musical current only they hear. Starfish cling to rocks. Fish in magnificent multi-colors are everywhere. Sunlight slices through the water, transmitting light to this magical underwater world.

Whatever life throws your way, you now have the sea to calm you down. You may be surfing through a major life adjustment or floating along a sea of serenity …. that's the ups and downs of life.

Be mindful of your journey. Pay attention to the highs and lows, the good times and the not-so-good times. The joy and the pain. Move gently with each wave.

As you go about your life, from this day forward, think of the sea. Carry its calm tide deep within you.

The wave

Imagine your breath as a surfboard.

Visualize your discomfort, anxiety or craving as a wave.

As the feeling grows, ride up the wave and then over, as the feelings recede, settling calmly in the still water.

If the feeling returns, again ride up the wave and then over as the feelings recede, settling calmly in the still water.

Just keep riding the waves as the feeling arises.

And finally, settle calmly in the still water.

Craving and anxiety typically come in waves and last only a few minutes, though seemingly longer. This visualization can be done over and over until you are calmer, or the craving has passed.

No. 27 of 56 Ways

Instead of reaching for something sweet mid-afternoon today, take three deep breaths. Poll your Triangle of Self-Awareness. Did the three breaths help you relax?

> **Meditation:** Welcome to 15 minutes of unguided meditation. When you finish today's meditation, you will be three-quarters of the way to the meditation time science tells us will changes your patterns of behavior.

Day 28

HALFWAY MARK

TODAY MARKS THE END OF your fourth week immersed in mindfulness, and we think by this time you are discovering two things:

1. That meditation, the foundation for living a mindful life, teaches you many life lessons that translate into….
2. Bringing mindfulness into every aspect of the rest of your day.

This week's focus was on the importance of communicating succinctly, with thought, intention and purpose. When you truly become aware of the power of your words, you begin to become impeccable with them, a concept so eloquently outlined in one of our favorite books, *The Four Agreements* by Don Miguel Ruiz. When you are truly impeccable with your words, you also become impeccable with your thoughts, and that leads to a calming of your inner critic.

Some of this week's lessons might not have hit a cord, but sometime soon you will be in a meeting or having a conversation that proves to be uncomfortable. We urge you that when this happens, review this week, and analyze exactly what happened and how you could have gotten the result you truly wanted.

A life lesson

For many of our clients, one of the lessons they think of often is Churchill and the polar bear. They say they often think of those two hugging each other and rolling around the snow, becoming friends, and if these two divergent personalities could get along, they can find a way to meet controversy by calming down.

Or sometimes, just recognizing that they are in the presence of an aggressive or toxic personality, they learn to walk away and never look back.

We wish this for you.

Reflections: Go back and re-read your contract. Commit again.

No. 28 of 56 Ways

Be quiet for five to 20 minutes. You can lie down or sit, gaze out the window, or take a slow, quiet walk. Just simply be.

> **Meditation:** We're holding at 15 minutes. Remember your anchors. And journal at the end of your meditation.

Week 5

Your thought for the week:

> *Your inner critic is simply the garbage you have accumulated during your life.*

Day 29

HELLO INNER CRITIC

WELCOME TO WEEK 5 – the halfway point in this book. We hope you are enjoying your journey so far. You have begun to start paying attention to what is going on internally and externally, becoming more aware and opening yourself up to untapped possibilities.

Next step!

Before you go any further, flip back to Day 4 and redo the Mindful Awareness Survey. Remember, answer with your gut, and please don't compare your answers to those you put down on Day 4 until you finish.

Some of your answers might be different; if they are, take a few minutes and think about why. Are you slowing down? Maybe you're a tad more aware of what is going on around you? Maybe you are now looking at a question in a different way, which brings about new understanding?

And now we start one of our favorite – and most difficult – topics…

The inner critic

Do you have one? Probably. Honestly, only one of our clients has said he doesn't have one.

Arianna Huffington calls hers "obnoxious roommate," and we think that title says it all.

Your inner critic is never kind (hence the term critic), s/he is often a bully, and often undermines your positive feelings about yourself and others. It erodes your:
- Self-esteem;
- Confidence;
- Personal and intimate relationships.

We define the inner critic as "The garbage you accumulate during your life."

Think back to your childhood, teen or young adult years. When you think about what people said to you, do you remember all the positive words or do the negative ones take center stage? Some of our clients remember harsh words a teacher said to them. Or something a parent said – usually to improve a behavior – but the way it was said or the words that were chosen were abrasive and left a permanent mark.

Those are the thoughts that can become the basis for what your inner critic says to you. When they become the words that you hear in your mind over and over, they become believable. They become the questions you ask yourself:
- Why did I….?
- Why should I….?
- Why didn't I….?
- Why couldn't I….?
- Why aren't I….?

Is it your conscience?

No! Your inner critic is not your conscience. Your conscience is an inner feeling or voice that acts as a guide to the rightness or wrongness of a behavior. It is your moral compass. It is your right versus wrong barometer. *Your inner critic is garbage and a liar!*

Meditation helps?

Absolutely! When you meditate you:
- Notice your thoughts.
- Make no judgments about your thoughts.

The more you meditate, the better able you become to notice your thoughts and make no judgments about them 24/7. It becomes part of your being.

Most importantly, you can identify garbage from conscience. Your thoughts become clearer. You become freer. Your life gets easier.

Plus, you understand how the judgments you have made all your life truly make you suffer.

No. 29 of 56 Ways

Chew one bite of food 20 times before swallowing. You can do this once or as many times as you like. And as you chew, listen to what your thoughts are saying. Did your inner critic come out to play? This can be a funny exercise. Or not, depending on the thoughts that arise.

Meditation: 15 minutes. Use an anchor – your breath, counting, visualization – to return to your breath when you notice your thoughts. Remember, make no judgments about any of your thoughts. Just breathe. Just be.

Day 30

INNER CRITIC: PART 2!

Did you think we would devote only a day to our inner critic? With some of our long-time clients, we devote months to the topic since a single lesson is never going to make that voice disappear. Oh, if only that were so.

Nor will it go away today after we delve into the topic some more. Meditation will help you become aware of what the inner critic is telling you, and with awareness will come curiosity, then disbelief, until you eventually realize that voice is a liar.

There are seven main types of inner critics. Some of us have a little of each, while others might only have one. See where yours fits in.

1. **Perfectionist** sets high standards for behavior and performance, not allowing for any mistakes. Often, you work on a project forever trying to get it perfect. You may also stop yourself from doing something of interest for fear that you won't be good enough.
2. **Inner Controller** tries to control your impulsive behavior – eating too many sweets, drinking too much alcohol, using drugs or stimulants – which is not bad except when it's your critic

speaking. Then, when you slip up, it can be harsh and shaming, attacking your willpower.
3. **Taskmaster** tells you that to be successful, you need to be disciplined and work exceptionally hard, which often leads to over-work and over-striving.
4. **Under-miner** tries to undermine your self-esteem and self-confidence, so you won't take risks or try and fail. It paralyzes you so you don't take action and feel worthless.
5. **Destroyer** makes pervasive attacks on your fundamental self-worth. It shames you deeply. It believes you shouldn't exist.
6. **Guilt-Tripper** attacks you for some specific action you have taken or not taken in the past, or for a repeated behavior that has been harmful to others or violates a deeply-held value – whether it was done deliberately or not. It makes you feel guilty and will never forgive you.
7. **Molder** tries to get you to fit a certain mold or act a certain way that derives from your family or culture. If you don't fit into the mold, it constantly makes you feel inadequate.

On the next page you'll have the chance to Define Your Inner Critic.

No. 30 of 56 Ways

Set alerts to ring throughout the day on your smartphone or timer. These are your reminders to take a few minutes to close your eyes and breathe. How does this make you feel? Poll your Triangle of Self-Awareness.

> **Meditation:** Still holding at 15 – at least for today!

DEFINE YOUR INNER CRITIC

Instructions: Answer each question by asking yourself, *"How often is this true for me?"* This is a thinking exercise and a way to look inward for a few minutes. There are no right or wrong answers – and you can tell that to your inner critic!

Scoring:

0–Never   1–Seldom   2–Sometimes   3–Frequently   4–Always

1. I feel like there is something wrong with me. ____

2. I set extremely high standards for myself. ____

3. I feel deeply ashamed of myself. ____

4. I feel terrible about myself when I am out of control. ____

5. When I think of trying something new and challenging, I give up before I begin. ____

6. I push myself to work very hard so I can achieve my goals. ____

7. I can't let go of things I've done or forgive myself. ____

8. I have a hard time feeling OK about myself when I am going against how I was programmed to act as child. ____

9. I burn up a great deal of effort trying to control my impulsive behaviors. ____

10. My self-confidence is so low I don't believe I can succeed at anything. ____

11. I beat myself up when I make a mistake. ____

12. I find it hard to start new projects because it is unacceptable to make mistakes even when I am just learning. ____

13. I feel crushed by a sense of worthlessness. ____

14. There is no end to the things I create for myself to do. ____

15. I have rigid standards for what I can eat and how much. ____

16. I believe that it is safer not to try than to fail. ____

17. I get anxious and self-critical when things don't come out perfectly. ____

18. I feel ashamed when I don't measure up to others' expectations. ____

19. I feel bad because I am too lazy to make it in the world. ____

20. I have a nagging feeling that I am morally bad. ____

21. I feel bad because I can't be what my family or culture expects of me. ____

22. I feel ashamed of my habits. ____

23. I spend too much time on projects trying to make them as good as possible. ____

24. I feel that I don't have what it takes to succeed. ____

25. I know who I ought to be, and I'm hard on myself when I act differently. ____

Day 31

INNER CRITIC: PART 3!

So now you have a pretty good idea of who your inner critic is, and how it works to undermine you.

Feeling overwhelmed? Do we have a meditation for you!

This is our suggestion on how to practice this meditation: Read it below, then visit our website, www.PathwayToMindfulness.com, Meditation tab, scroll down to audio meditations, "RAIN." After reading and listening to it, it will be yours forever, to be used whenever you are feeling overwhelmed and need a kind dose of self-compassion.

RAIN

Imagine that it is a warm summer day, and you are sitting on a porch, either in a comfy chair with lots of cushions, a rocking chair or porch swing. The porch is white with a light blue ceiling, mimicking the sky. You close your eyes and can smell the just-mowed grass, the flowers in a vase by your side and the gentle rain that has just started to fall.

As you begin to breathe, you think of the word **RAIN.**

R: Recognize what is going on. What has made you overwhelmed?

A: Allow the experience to be here, just as it is.

I: Investigate with kindness and curiosity. No judgment. No harsh words. Just think about why you are overwhelmed.

N: Natural awareness is now yours, and it comes from not identifying with the experience. It comes with just investigating and being kind to yourself.

This meditation can be done over and over, until you are calmer and the feeling of being overwhelmed is subsiding.

Inner critic returns

With a lovely, visual meditation under your belt, it's time to go back to your inner critic, but in a gentler way. What follows is the first half of our plan for tuning down the inner critic's voice.

1. **Awareness.** For many, the inner critic is there in the background, spewing its hate without us even realizing it. But as soon as you begin to notice these thoughts, then you are able to take action to make them go away – or imagine this –say only nice and benevolent things about you. In case you haven't made the connection – you learn to notice your thoughts in meditation, and this noticing eventually begins to spill over into the rest of your day. Ergo, meditating, daily, is key.
2. **No judgment.** Noticing your thoughts without judgment is what you do in meditation. We just gave you another reason to meditate, although by now we hope you love meditation so much, it's become an important part of your day.
3. **Perfection.** We all really need to let this go. Perfection is unattainable and believing this is freeing. When we talk about

perfection it is more than what you expect of yourself; it is also what you require from others.
4. **Comparisons.** Once you start comparing yourself, your possessions, your lifestyle, etc., to others, you start to diminish yourself. Honestly, no one knows what goes on behind the closed doors of others. Pay attention to your life and concentrate on what you have. Even in times of distress, most of us have so much.
5. **Naming rights.** Give your critical inner voice a name, but not a pretty or sexy name. Make it silly, like Ned the Nag, Gross Gremlin, Perfect Polly – you think of what works best for you. And start talking back to that voice. Ask: "Perfect Polly, why are you so mean?" Would you ever say the things your critical inner voice tells you to a friend? Not if you want to keep that friend.
6. **Pause.** The next time that voice speaks, pause. Take a breath. Do not get sucked into an internal debate.
7. **Curiosity:** Time to look at what is really going on and why that voice is speaking. Poll your triangle: is it a thought, emotion or physical sensation that started the conversation? Are you tired? Angry? Insecure? Stressed? There are so many reasons why that voice is speaking.
8. **Inhale:** Peace.
9. **Exhale:** Any negative thoughts your voice was saying.
10. **Change:** Now make the thoughts in your head positive.

Day 31 of 56 Ways

At lunch, change your environment. Then take a few moments, be present in the experience, noticing the sights, sounds, smells, as you eat. Is your critical inner voice eating with you, or were you able to say, "go away."

> **Meditation:** You are up to 16 minutes today. We have found that once our clients get to 16 minutes, many just up it to 20 minutes. No pressure. If you want to stay at 16 minutes for a few days, it's fine. Remember, this is your meditation.

Day 32

INNER CRITIC: PART 4!

CONTRACT SIGNING TIME! BUT THIS is a good one. It's a pledge you are making between you and your inner critic – a lifetime contract that we hope you keep in a prominent place and refer to often.

INNER CRITIC CONTRACT

Dear Inner Critic,

I've spent entirely too much time over the years listening to you.

I'm kindly suggesting we take a break. A permanent one. A forever break, 'cause I don't need you anymore!

Love,

Second half of taming the inner critic

Now when _____ (fill in your inner critic's name) comes out to play, use these tips for shooing those thoughts away.

1. **Put negative stuff in a small box**: Imagine a small box and insert all negative self-talk into it. Close it up. Tape it shut. Whatever! Even if the problem is monumental, envisioning a small box makes the problem seem smaller.
2. **Power of possible thinking**: Positive thinking is sometimes impossible. But possible thinking? Make your thoughts possible. Instead of saying "I am too stupid to do that," say "The task is complicated, but if I take it in steps, it will be done." Or saying, "I am a fat cow" versus "I want to lose 10 pounds and I know how to do that." Then make a game plan.
3. **Choose to be kind to *you***: Question your inner thoughts. Ask a lot of questions – until you start doubting what your critical inner voice is saying. Dilute the conversation and you win.
4. **Spin, spin, spin**: Notice the difference: "I am stupid" versus "Boy, did I feel stupid." The former describes who you are, which is not a representation of your true self. The second simply says that you are feeling stupid at that time. We all feel inadequate at times throughout life. But that should not define you.
5. **Ask: What would my best friend say?** We have said it before: You say things to yourself you would never say to a friend. Speak to yourself as you would speak to your best friend.
6. **Embrace your imperfections**: Stop holding yourself up to high standards. Everyone has flaws — they build character and make you unique. Be willing to mess up. And then move on.

Positivity

Positivity to self is powerful, but often hard. Can you write down your positive traits?

Let's try. Write down as many as you can think of. We're giving you a whole page for this exercise because you should be able to fill it up. Probably not all today, but we suggest you keep this list in a place where you can see it often – we keep ours in our journal – and add to it when you are having a good day. On bad days, refer to this list often.

Your Positive Traits!

No. 32 of 56 Ways

When you are finally home for the night, change your clothes, signaling a transition in your day. Pay attention to what you wore today and what clothes you are changing into. Really look at your clothes. We usually carefully choose our daytime outfits but the clothes we wear at night – usually no time at all. Do you like your nighttime clothes? Do they make you feel comfy? Perhaps sexy? Do they feel good on your skin? Maybe it's time for a shopping trip to find something that really makes you feel good about you.

> **Meditation:** 16 minutes of meditation today, paying attention to your breath and how important it is for your life.

Day 33

FORGIVING YOURSELF

FORGIVING YOURSELF IS A NECESSARY component for turning down and softening the inner critic.

To blame yourself is human nature. You blame yourself:
- For things done or not done;
- For saying something unkind to family or friends;
- For hating yourself for something you said or wrote in an email.
- Etc., etc., etc.

Reflections: Pen/pencil time!

What are some things that you can't forgive yourself for?
_____
_____
_____

Do you agree: Forgiving yourself and learning from past mistakes is important for your health and well-being? Probably yes.

Self-forgiveness is a difficult but manageable feat if you take a mindful approach. The good news is that it gets easier as you become more skillful.

How do we forgive ourselves?

1. **Know that you are not the first person who has made this mistake.** Most of us take things personally, to a fault. But you're not that unique – others make or have made the same mistake. When you begin to understand that no one is immune to being unskillful, you can begin to take it a little less personally. That is the first step in forgiving yourself.
2. **Understand that it's in the past.**
    - It's over, so long as you are not continuing the behavior. It is in the past.
    - Acknowledge its presence and then remind yourself that you made a mistake, but that was the past and you are going to learn from it. Grow. Move forward. This will free you to be more skillful in the present.
3. **Adopt a learning mindset.**
    - Forgive yourself for the past transgression. But, investigate, *with kindness,* how or why you made this error, or if it was even an error on your part at all.
    - Ask yourself: "What might I do differently next time?" Then invite yourself to begin again.
4. **Going forward:** Develop a conscious intention on how you want things to be, how you want to be or respond moving forward.

Remember: This is a process that takes patience, determination and persistence.

The old stories and habits of self-blame will creep back into your mind, leading you back toward your old unforgiving ways that don't serve you well. When this happens, invite yourself to begin the process of self-forgiveness again.

No. 33 of 56 Ways

Look at a past event that you wrote about a few minutes ago, one that has been haunting you. Sit quietly, take a few breaths and settle. Use the tools above, take your time and – with focus and attention – work through each of the steps. Find peace and forgiveness, free yourself to live in the present and move forward. You know we are going to ask you to think of your Triangle of Self-Awareness during this exercise but it's an important part of healing.

> **Meditation:** 16 to 20 minutes: Meet yourself wherever you are comfortable.

Day 34

BODY SCAN

Our meditation style is primarily unguided silent meditation, but today you will be practicing a guided meditation that once you listen to a few times, can easily transform into an unguided meditation.

What does a body scan do for you? Through focus, attention and awareness, you learn to connect your physical sensations, thoughts and emotions, the Triangle of Self-Awareness. Some meditation styles use this guided meditation exclusively as the primary meditation technique. For us it is another tool, a way to bring mindfulness into your life.

During the body scan you will experience each part of your body, as it is, aware but absent any judgment about what you feel or don't feel. You'll also relax those body parts and release any tension or emotions you become aware of. This exercise builds focus, attention and calmness of mind and body.

The body scan helps teach you how to manage pain and discomfort in the body. It teaches you to be aware of physical sensations and linger, without judgment, and then let them dissolve while moving your attention and focus to another part of your body.

You can read through this once, or simply listen to it on our website, www.Pathwaytomindfulness.com, Meditation tab, scroll down to Audio meditations, titled Body scan.

Since this is a longer meditation, a blanket or sweater can keep you warm and cozy.

Posture:

Lying down. This prone position is the most common way the body scan is taught. For comfort, some meditators put a support under their knees and/or their head.

Astronaut position. A personal favorite, which may be more comfortable than lying down. As a visualization, think of astronauts sitting in their rocket chairs – with the seat tipped back to the floor and legs above. You can emulate this with your back and head on the floor, thighs at a 90-degree angle, and calves and feet resting on a chair or sofa.

This is easier on most people's back than lying down, and quite comfortable.

Seated. Sit on a comfortable chair or couch. If on a chair, we would suggest that it have arms as some people unconsciously lean over during this meditation. We wouldn't want you to fall! If sitting, try not to slouch.

A common and sometimes embarrassing effect of a body scan is sleeping on the job! When we teach classes, if there are more than four students, at least one, usually two, will drift off to sleep and then waken a few minutes later. How bad is this? Hmm, seems to us your body is telling you something: You're tired and this meditation is relaxing you. Nothing wrong here: No need to judge or feel embarrassed since you're simply nourishing your body. The upside? Many people use a silent, self-directed body scan to help them get to sleep.

Guided body scan

Take a comfortable position. Close your eyes, lower them, or soften your gaze. Breathe, just breathe.

Inhale, and as you exhale soften your body. Breathe. As you exhale sink into the mat or chair. Settle, relax. Release all tension in your body while staying in a state of full awareness.

We invite you to bring your attention to your feet, becoming aware of whatever sensations are there. Perhaps warmth or coolness. If you are registering a blank as you tune in, then just experience nothing. **Stay with this for six to 10 breaths.**

Now as you breathe in, imagine your breath moving in your nose, all the way down to your feet, and then when it reaches your feet, begin your outbreath and let it move all the way up your body and out your nose. You are breathing in from your nose and then breathing out from your feet. **Stay with this for six to 10 breaths.**

On the next breath, as you exhale, let your feet dissolve from your mind's eye.

Become aware of your shins and calf muscles, all the sensations in your lower legs. Not just on the surface, but down into the bones, experiencing and accepting what you feel here. **Stay with this for six to 10 breaths.**

Now breathing into them, then breathing out from them. **Stay with this for six to 10 breaths.**

On the next exhalation let go of your lower legs as you relax into the mat or chair.

Moving now into the thighs. If there is any tension, just noticing that, and relaxing. Perhaps you can feel your pulse, the feel of the blood flow. Linger. Now breathe into and out from the thighs. **Stay with this for six to 10 breaths.**

Then let your thighs dissolve and relax.

Breathe. Relaxed, but in a state of full awareness. **Stay with this for six to 10 breaths.**

Shift your attention to your pelvis now. From one hip to the other. Notice your buttocks in contact with the mat or chair. The sensations of contact and of weight. Become aware of the region of the genitals, whatever sensations, or lack of sensations you are experiencing. **Stay with this for six to 10 breaths.**

Now direct your breath down into your pelvis, breathing with the entirety of your pelvis. And as you breathe out, moving the breath back up through your body and out your nose, let your pelvis soften, release all tension as you sink even deeper into a state of relaxed awareness and stillness. Totally present in each moment. Content to just be, and to just be right here as you are, right now. **Stay with this for six to 10 breaths.**

Direct your attention to your lower back, just experiencing your back as it is. This is an area that is often tense or in a state of discomfort. Let your breath penetrate and move into every part of your lower back on the in breath. And on the out breath, just let any tension, any tightness, any holding on, just flow out as much as it will. **Stay with this for six to 10 breaths.**

And then let go of your lower back. **Stay with this for six to 10 breaths.**

Now move your attention into your upper back, just feeling the sensations in your upper back. You may even feel your ribcage expand, in back as well as in front, with each in breath. If you sense any tightness, fatigue or discomfort in this part of your body, just let it dissolve and move out with the out breath, as you let go and sink even deeper into stillness and relaxation. **Stay with this for six to 10 breaths.**

Shift your attention to your belly, experience the rise and fall of your belly as you breathe, feeling the movements of your diaphragm, that muscle separating your belly from your chest. Experience your chest as it expands on the in breath and deflates on the out breath.

If you can, tune into the rhythmic beating of your heart within your chest. Feel it if you can. Try to feel the lungs expanding on either side of your heart.

Just experience your chest, your belly, as you lie here, the muscles on the chest wall, the breasts, the entirety of the front of your body. And now just let this region dissolve into relaxation as well. **Stay with this for six to 10 breaths.**

Move your attention now to your fingertips on both hands, becoming aware of the sensations in the tips of your fingers and thumbs. Can you feel some pulsations from the blood flow, perhaps a dampness or a warmth, or whatever you feel, just feel your fingers. **Stay with this for six to 10 breaths.**

Expand your awareness to include the palms of your hands, the backs of your hands and your wrists, here again perhaps picking up the pulsations of the arteries in your wrists as the blood flows to and from your hands **Stay with this for six to 10 breaths.**

Become aware of the forearms, now the elbows, any and all sensations regardless of what they are. **Stay with this for six to 10 breaths.**

Allow the field of your awareness to include the upper arms, right up to your shoulders. Just experiencing your shoulders, and if there is any tension, breathe into your shoulders and arms, letting that tension dissolve as you breathe out. **Stay with this for six to 10 breaths.**

Now let your arms dissolve from your mind's eye. All the way from your fingertips, right to your shoulders, as you sink even deeper into a state of relaxed awareness. Just be present in each moment. Let go of whatever thoughts come up or any impulses to move, just experience yourself in this moment. **Stay with this for six to 10 breaths.**

Focus your attention on your neck and throat. Feel this part of your body, experiencing what it feels like, perhaps when you swallow, when you breathe. And then letting it go. Letting it relax and dissolve from your mind's eye. **Stay with this for six to 10 breaths.**

Become aware of your face now. Focus on the jaw and the chin, just experiencing them as they are. Become aware of your lips and your mouth, your cheeks, and now your nose, feeling the breath as it moves in and out at the nostrils.

Now be aware of your eyes. And the entire region around your eyes and eyelids. If there's any tension, letting it leave as you exhale. Notice your forehead, then letting it soften to let go of stored emotions. Now the temples. **Stay with this for six to 10 breaths.**

If you sense any emotion associated with the tension or feelings in your face, just be aware of that. Breathe in and as you exhale, let your face dissolve into relaxation and stillness.

And now become aware of your ears, and back and top of your head. Now let your whole face and head relax. For now, just letting it be as it is. Let it be still and neutral. Relaxed and at peace. **Stay with this for six to 10 breaths.**

As you inhale let your breath move through your entire body in whatever way feels natural for you. And then exhale from your whole body. **Stay with this for 10 breaths.**

Just breathe. All your muscles are in a deep state of relaxation. And your mind is simply aware of energy, of this flow of breath. **Stay with this for 10 breaths.**

Experience your entire body breathing. Sinking deeper and deeper into a state of stillness, of deep relaxation. Totally awake with complete awareness. **Stay with this for 10 breaths.**

Allow yourself to feel whole. In touch with your essential self in a realm of silence, of stillness, of peace. **Stay with this for 10 breaths.**

Notice this stillness is healing. Allow the world to be as it is, beyond your personal fears and concerns, beyond the desires of your mind to want everything to be a certain way. **Stay with this for 10 breaths.**

See yourself as complete, right now, as you are. **Stay with this for 10 breaths.**

As the exercise comes to an end, bring your awareness back to your body again, feeling the whole of it. **Stay with this for 10 breaths.**

Move your fingers and toes as you continue to come back to the body. Breathe. **Stay with this for six to 10 breaths.**

May you be happy. May you be healthy. May you ride the waves of your life. May you live your life in peace and with ease no matter what you are given. **Stay with this for six to 10 breaths.**

Allow this calmness and this centeredness to remain with you as you begin to move now.

Congratulate yourself on having taken the time to nourish yourself in this way. This state of relaxation and clarity is available to you by simply paying attention to your breath. Any time, any place, any moment, no matter what's happening in your day. Let your breath be a source of constant strength and energy for you as you release from this experience.

No. 34 of 56 Ways

Practice self-care throughout the day, starting with your meals. Eat only foods that you love today. Consider making a new recipe that is calling your name. And then savor each bite. Notice your Triangle of Self-Awareness. How do your foods make your body feel? Your thoughts? Your emotions?

> **Meditation:** 16 minutes today. We know the body scan takes time, but it is a guided meditation – at least today. If you do the body scan meditation often, eventually it becomes an unguided meditation because you know what to do. But today, 16 minutes of unguided meditation is prescribed. Or 20. Meet yourself where you are.

Day 35

REVIEW

Had enough talk about your inner critic for now? We know there's been a lot of information to digest this week, including some exercises to do to keep that inner voice of yours controlled. It is such an important topic and one that most of us never think about.

Understanding your critical inner voice and building awareness about what it is saying is an important step to take on your mindful journey.

Why?

This week you learned that in most cases, your critical inner voice becomes background talk that unfortunately shapes the way you feel about yourself. When you are constantly bombarded with the negative – without realizing this is happening – it leaves you open to a life of self-doubt and insecurity. It can also lead to bad manners and behavior.

Want proof?

Consider the narcissist. According to the Mayo Clinic: Narcissistic personality disorder is a mental condition in which people have an inflated sense of their own importance, a deep need for excessive attention and admiration, troubled relationships, and a lack of empathy for others. *Behind this mask of extreme confidence lies a fragile self-esteem that's vulnerable to the slightest criticism.*

Who would have thought?

We encourage you to think about your thoughts, and when they go haywire, become aware, notice and investigate with curiosity, and then try to change that recording to a more positive one.

Reflections: Go back and re-read your contract. Commit again.

No. 35 of 56 Ways

Bring out your positive traits list. If you're having a good day, add to your list. If it's a not-so-good day, read it over and believe in every item on the list. That's you. Glorious you.

> **Meditation:** To celebrate the end of the week, up your meditation to 17 minutes. Rejoice! You're almost at 20 minutes a day, the time science says will change your patterns of behavior. And look how far you've already come. Just imagine the possibilities!

Week 6

Your thought for the week:

> *The more you love yourself,
> the better able you will be to love others.*

Day 36

YOU ARE NOT YOUR THOUGHTS

Here's a thought. You don't have to control your thoughts; you just have to stop letting them control you.

Thoughts can hurt, but only if you give them power.

Mindfulness teaches you awareness without judgment. This lets you:
- **Step outside of yourself:** You become the observer and look at your thoughts as a fleeting event. You don't become attached to them.
- **Suspend judgment.** Having horrible, evil thoughts about someone? Who doesn't? The mind's job is to think and, oh boy, does it. But the thought itself is only that, a thought. Don't judge yourself by it.
- **Choose your thoughts.** You can determine what you want to think about and let go of other thoughts. Don't let them take over your mind.

As you grow in mindfulness you start to untangle your thoughts and you:
- Minimize emotional reactions, responding instead.
- Become more authentic as you let go of your thoughts and fears about how other people are perceiving you. You begin to not worry about whether they accept you or not. You are free to just be. The following sounds harsh but is something to consider "I don't care enough about you to care about what you think." You determine who makes the cut, and ask yourself, "Who do I care enough about to let them factor into my thoughts."
- Through meditation you learn to distance yourself from judging your thoughts. And that's when you stop listening and start paying attention to you.

Analogy: you are lowering the sound of the TV that is constantly playing in your mind. Your purpose is not to eliminate the sound but to improve it.

No. 36 of 56 Ways

Turning down your negative thoughts

1. **Recognize the thought**, for example, *Life is never going to get better.* Just recognize this thought – whatever the thought may be – that is forming in your mind.
2. **Relax the body, release the thinking**: Negative thoughts make your body react – the fight/flight/freeze reaction. Breathe deeply to relax. Use your out breath to release the tension and any negative thoughts. On the in breath, focus on peace.
3. **Flip the conversation in your head**: Through breathing, you created space between you and your negative thoughts. Now think positive thoughts. Ask yourself:
    - *What's good right now?*
    - *What's going on that's good in my life?*
    - *Am I in a safe place right now?*
    - *Perhaps think about some friends you can count on.*

Just recognize some good things in your life and linger on them for a bit.

The more you do this exercise, the more you will begin to change your negative thoughts.

> **Meditation:** Holding at 17 minutes. But if you want to try 20, go for it!

Day 37

THE VAGUS NERVE

Remember the last time a scary or super-stressful event made your stomach flip, or you suffered the loss of a loved one or furry friend that made your heart ache?

That reaction is generated by your vagus nerve, part of your parasympathetic nervous system and the largest nerve in the parasympathetic network.

The autonomic or involuntary nervous system consists of two complementary systems, sympathetic and parasympathetic. Together they manage your daily living functions absent your conscious input like breathing and heart beats.

They are unlike your somatic or voluntary nervous system that initiates actions like walking or opening and closing our hands.

The sympathetic nervous system is tied to your fight/flight/freeze reactions, and its job is to increase energy by raising your heart rate and blood pressure. The parasympathetic system's job is to conserve energy and is rest and digestion oriented, lowering your heart rate, increasing saliva and managing the digestive cycle. It is also critical to glandular activity, sexual arousal and more.

The vagus nerve is connected to the brain, ears, larynx, heart and stomach. The most extreme vagal response impacts your cognitive function, can make you unable to hear or recognize what's being said, and leaves you speechless with a heartache and upset stomach.

Why is this important?

Vagal tone is a measure of the responsiveness of the vagus nerve. While it causes the phenomenon noted above, it has a powerful upside: It stimulates and strengthens soothing hormones such as oxytocin, and happy hormones, including dopamine and endorphins.

People with strong vagal tone are also healthier, have robust immune systems and better interpersonal relationships.

Vagal tone is typically established during the first year of life. Before you start thinking there is nothing you can do about your vagal tone, we have great news to share: Science has proven that meditation boosts vagal tone, no matter your age!

No matter how poor your vagal tone is, by the time you finish this program your vagal tone will have received a real boost and will continue to grow as you meditate.

No. 37 of 56 Ways

Simple acts of kindness stimulate happy hormones. Practice a few simple acts of kindness today. They can be as simple as saying hello and a kind word to a grocery clerk or other stranger. Perhaps write a note to a distant friend.

Then notice how you feel. Poll your Triangle of Self-Awareness. Notice the happy emotion and see if you can feel a warmth in your heart and body, that your thoughts are positive.

Practice simple acts of kindness often – daily. A day without an act of kindness is like a day without sunshine. *The more you practice kindness the more kindness becomes part of your being.*

> **Meditation:** 17 minutes is the minimum now; 20 minutes is certainly doable.

Day 38

LOVE OF SELF

Do you treat yourself with love and kindness? Some philosophers and theologians say that if you don't love yourself, then it's hard – if not impossible – for you to love other people.

We think that is a bit harsh and soften those words, saying that the more self-love you have, the better able you are to show love to others. We are not talking about becoming narcissistic or ego driven. We are talking about self-care, putting your oxygen mask on first before you can help anyone else.

Reflections: Pen/pencil time!

When answering each question think broadly – people, places, events, anything that is part of your life, or you would like to bring into or remove from your life.

1. What nourishes me? What makes me feel alive, involved, interested – firmly anchored in the present?

2. What depletes me? What makes me want to hide under a pillow, not present in the moment?

3. What can I do to increase those things that nourish me? Be specific.

4. What can I do to decrease those things that deplete my energy? Be specific.

5. What can I let go of? And how could I do that? Be specific.

This is such an important exercise that we invite you to work on this over the next few weeks, as you go through your life and identify more things that nourish or deplete. Too often we take no notice of these people, places or events, and just go about life accepting that this is the way life is.

It is especially important to identify those things that deplete your energy and spirit. Once you become aware, then you can figure out the steps you need to do to fill up on what nourishes you most.

No. 38 of 56 Ways

Pay attention to your inner critic as you are thinking about the things that deplete your energy. What is your inner critic saying? Change the negative conversation to a more positive one. Say to yourself: "I need to be kinder and more compassionate to myself. I need to treat me as I treat others."

> **Meditation:** Between 17 and 20 minutes.

Day 39

A MATTER OF TIME

Mindfulness teacher Thich Nhat Hanh uses an expanded definition of diet to not only include what we eat and drink but what we consume with all our senses.

We love that definition, because all too often it is your expanded diet that leads you to fill your life with things that deplete rather than nourish. He also talks about the suffering caused by unmindful consumption and how this impacts your sense of well-being and consciousness.

You guessed it: Today we are still talking about self-care. You began this exploration yesterday, beginning to identify the things in your life that nourish and those that deplete. We are offering some interesting ways to look at this subject, and to what the father of Western Mindfulness, Jon Kabat-Zinn, wrote in "Full Catastrophe Living" – the tyranny of time.

At Pathway to Mindfulness, we often hear people complain that they simply cannot find 20 minutes each day to meditate. That's when we introduce this concept, and we think right now is the time, as we begin to hit that all-important 20 minutes. You really do have the time. You just might need to rearrange some things in your present life.

What follows are ways to free yourself from the tyranny of time, adapted from Kabat-Zinn. Honestly, don't you love that phrase?

1. **Remind yourself that time is the product of thoughts.** Minutes and hours were originally agreed upon so humans could meet, communicate and work in harmony. Think about two ways you could spend an hour: Having a root canal or reading your favorite book. The latter might seem like minutes while the former, half a day. Time is relative.

   You get 24 hours a day to organize your life. How you use that time and what you do with it makes all the difference in whether you see your life as never having enough, too little, or just the right amount of time. Awareness of what you are trying to accomplish and your expectations of yourself need to come into play here.

2. **Live in the present more of the time.** Fifty-three to 60 percent of our time is spent thinking about the past or worrying about the future. That's tons of wasted time, not to mention how it's a breeding ground for depression and anxiety to flourish. When you drop out of automatic pilot, and really pay attention to the task at hand, you will get more done. With awareness also comes the ability to identify non-nourishing items, and with that awareness often comes adjustments.

   We're not suggesting that you forget all the wonderful memories that truly weave the stories of your life. But if you do think about them, be aware that you are doing so and savor and enjoy each wonderful feeling that surfaces.

   We're also understand that you have to plan for the future. But again, do so in the present, with total awareness.

Live in the present moment. If you are in a hurry, do so with awareness. Pay attention to your breathing and how fast movement affects your body – remember the Triangle of Self-Awareness! And when the hurrying is over, give yourself time to recover.

Your life will always have challenges. It is how you respond to each that will determine your state of mind and health.

3. **Devote some time each day to meditate.** You knew this was coming, but it's so very important. Some of our busiest clients find 20 minutes daily to meditate because they know how it has changed their lives and that they can't live without it. They put it right up there with basic needs: food, clothing and shelter – adding meditation to the list.

And that is what we wish for you.

Schedule it into your calendar. If it's scheduled, then you have no excuse. Maybe it means getting up a few minutes earlier, which could mean going to bed a few minutes earlier at night. Life is all about choice and compromise.

4. **Simplify your life.** Prioritize the things that you need in your life and consciously choose to give up other things that are not nourishing your being. This a recipe for success. One of our clients gave up Facebook because she was tired of seeing everyone's *perfect* life. Another gave up a board position because he found the experience too negative. Another stopped watching the morning news because it was not only depressing her, but it was making her crazy – her words, not ours!

We can all become addicted to sensory bombardment, constantly checking our texts, emails and social media. Or how about TV? Or exercise, which is wonderful but for some it becomes an addiction. What affect does all this have on a body? *Stress!*

No. 39 of 56 ways

1. Identify the stress factors in your life.
2. Gradually decrease the stress and toxicity in your life.
3. Start adding nourishing events.

See: It's as simple as 1, 2, 3! Not really, but it's a start.

> **Meditation:** 18 minutes is now the minimum. Feel free to up it to 20 minutes.

Day 40

SELF-WORTH

The Dalai Lama was teaching a group of U.S. therapists, and one asked him: how do you handle poor self-worth, self-hatred?

His reply: Why would anyone not love themselves? Why would anyone hate themselves?

And although he speaks very good English, the interpreter got involved because the Dali Lama was confused. He finally told the group that this must be a mistake. And then he asked: Have you ever hated yourself? Or did not feel worthy? Every hand went up.

They told him that they all suffer from shame, guilt and feel unworthy, and for many of them it is the default mode in their lives.

His answer: They need to practice more loving kindness and self-compassion.

But all too often that critical inner voice is in the way.

How do we mindfully boost our self-worth?

Complete the following exercise, writing down your negative thoughts. When you write something out, you are creating space in your thinking, which separates your negative thoughts and emotions. It also provides time for you to reflect if this judgment is correct or not. Because it is written down and processed, you no longer have to worry about it. At least that's the intention!

You will notice that the exercise also asks you if these thoughts are habits. It also asks how this thought makes you feel as you identify the negative thought. You can ultimately notice that thoughts are transient and not fact.

And the final question – do you know the source? Could it be like so many other negative thoughts – something that has been ingrained in your psyche since childhood, all too often becoming a habit? And when you investigate it with loving kindness, you might arrive at the conclusion that this old habit is no longer effective.

Reflections: Pen/pencil time!

See how many negative thoughts you can identify. Keep coming back to this exercise as a negative thought pops into your head.

My negative thought:
_____
_____
_____

Is it a habit?
_____
_____
_____

How does it make me feel?
___
___
___

The source?
___
___
___

No. 40 of 56 Ways

Understand your triggers. If being late for appointments makes you anxious, leave earlier. If lines and traffic make you uneasy, practice breathing or look around and notice things you never would have seen if you didn't take the time to look. Live in the present.

> **Meditation:** 18-20 minutes today.

Day 41

LOVING KINDNESS

WE HOPE YOU ARE GETTING the message that it is imperative for you to show yourself love, kindness and self-care.

Earlier in this book we asked you to say: "I love you (fill in your name)" first thing every morning, and last thing at night. We hope you are still saying those four little words at least twice each day. We also suggested you follow those words with five deep breaths. This is a forever exercise!

Today, we are going to introduce the Loving Kindness Meditation (Metta Bhavana in Sanskrit). This meditation is how we begin our morning unguided meditation because we feel it is so important to our being as mindful coaches and meditation teachers.

There are four distinct sections of the meditation, each with a purpose and equally important.

The first stage is to bring loving kindness to self. A few of our clients have a hard time doing this at first, but we encourage them to try because the difficulty proves that they need it most.

The second stage is to bring loving kindness to someone who supports you or who needs a little boost in their lives.

The third stage is the hardest for some – to offer loving kindness to someone who has brought you pain or difficulty.

The fourth and last stage is to bring loving kindness to the greater community – your town, your state, the world.

You can simply read through the meditation, or listen to it on our website, www.Pathwaytomindfulness.com, Meditation tab, scroll down to Audio meditations, titled, Loving Kindness. This meditation does not take the place of your 20-minute unguided meditation until you say the words yourself in meditation.

Ours is a simple version and we encourage our clients to add anything that they might need, for example, May I be kind or May I live with ease. There are no rules in meditation. Make it as personal as you like. Each phase is said three times.

Loving Kindness Meditation

We start with ourselves.
May I be happy
May I be healthy
May I ride the waves of my life
May I live in peace
No matter what I am given
Pause and notice the feelings that arise....

Now, offer loving kindness to someone who supports you.
May you be happy
May you be healthy
May you ride the waves of your life
May you live in peace
No matter what you are given

Pause and notice the feelings that arise....

Turn your attention now to someone with whom you have difficulty.
May you be happy
May you be healthy
May you ride the waves of your life
May you live in peace
No matter what you are given
Pause and notice the feelings that arise....

And now bring to mind the broader community.
May we be happy
May we be healthy
May we ride the waves of our lives
May we live in peace
No matter what we are given
Pause and notice the feelings that arise....

No. 41 of 56 Ways

Tell yourself first thing in the morning and last thing at night: "I love you (fill in your name)." Follow this with five deep breaths, morning and night. Do this every day, forever. If you have a hard time loving yourself at your present age, start with loving your infant self and gradually increase your age until you reach your present age.

We have included this today as a refresher, for many reasons. First, you might have forgotten to do this as the weeks progressed. Second, we mentioned it in this lesson. And third, we feel this is critical for leading a mindful life. These four little words, which once our clients truly believe, begins the healing process.

Meditation: 18 to 20 minutes today.

Day 42

WEEK'S WRAP-UP

This week we looked inward, making the case that you need to put your oxygen mask on first before you can help anyone else. Today, let's have some fun because this week we've been concentrating on self-reflection, which can often wear us out.

Quiz time:

1. Thoughts can hurt but only if:

    a. you ignore them;
    b. you give them power.

2. People with strong vagal tone are:

    a. healthier, happier with better interpersonal relationships;
    b. lonely and depressed.

3. To break the tyranny of time:

    a. Spend more time in the present moment;
    b. Think about the past and the future more often to learn from your mistakes.

4. The Loving Kindness meditation is all about:

    a. You;
    b. Has four stages.

5. We boost our self-worth by:

    a. identifying our negative thoughts;
    b. ignoring our negative thoughts.

Answers: 1b; 2a; 3a; 4b; 5a.

All about you.

We invite you to fill this out, and then ask someone who cares about you to fill it out, too. If their rating is lower than yours, ask them to share specific examples. If you want, you can do this once a month to see if you are making any changes.

1 = rarely   2 = sometimes   3 = frequently

1. You raise and never lower the self-esteem of others. _____

2. You work outside your comfort zone to help others as much or even more than yourself. _____

3. You give equal effort to a fair decision that you either agree or disagree with. _____

4. You ask for help. _____

5. You quickly and sincerely thank someone for their help. _____

6. You quickly offer help without someone asking for it. _____

7. You fully forgive after you've been hurt. _____

8. You quickly forget after you forgive and move on. _____

9. You recognize and apologize when you've let someone down. _____

10. You congratulate someone on an achievement or good fortune – and mean it. _____

11. You give more to the world than you take from it. _____

11–16 = You may feel entitled and are probably more of a taker than a giver.

17–24 = You are a decent person but there is room for improvement.

25–33 = People are blessed to call you a friend or have you in their lives.

Reflection: Go back and re-read your contract. Commit again.

No. 42 of 56 Ways:

Become more patient, which is easier said than done. Become curious. Look inward and determine how your impatience affects your body. Let it go. Becoming more patient is freeing and delicious!

> **Meditation:** 19-20 minutes.

Week 7

Your thought for the week:

> *Do something this week that your future self will thank you for – forever.*

Day 43

SPOONSFUL OF LOVE

Co-author Bill Van Ollefen is presenting this lesson, because, as you will see, it is very personal. It is a lesson he was taught nearly 20 years ago that changed his life, and we feel can change yours, too.

Bill's story:

Lying in a hospital bed the morning after my third major spinal reconstruction surgery in 20 months, I woke to see a physical therapist at the foot of my bed. Let's call him Chuck. He cheerily smiled and said "good morning" while reading my chart and his therapy orders. Looking at my name, then face, I saw a flash of recognition in his eyes. "I know you," he said, "I've been your post-op therapist before." He read on, then frowned and looking up said, "Twice before. Why are you here? You shouldn't be here."

The first post-op session after this type of surgery is brutal. Pain, drugs, IVs and wires, hoses, monitors and they expect – no, make –you get out of bed and begin therapy. At the session's end I lay in bed shaking, in pain and tears. Chuck said good job and he'd see me after lunch for my next round of therapy.

The next therapy session was worse than the first, but I pushed through it, hard-guy style, with him trying to reign in my inner maniac. "Good job again" he said but added: "We really need to talk about some things tomorrow."

Chuck came back the next morning, pulled up a chair next to my bed, and asked me how my recovery from my last surgery had gone. Proudly I told him how I had returned to work four weeks earlier than anticipated, beginning with a 10-day business trip that included multiple cities on two continents. I told him that my golf game still suffered, and while I liked to walk the course and carry my bag, I lamented that my endurance wasn't up to snuff quite yet.

He sighed, then told me I was here by choice. Eyes wide I exclaimed, "*What?* Seriously?"

Reaching into his bag he took out 20 plastic spoons and stacked them neatly, side by side, on my tray. He said: "I'd like you to think of these 20 spoons as representing your available life-energy for the day. Each activity consumes a part of it. You can't borrow from tomorrow's energy, nor can you really save from one day to the next. Let's have a look at how your day went yesterday."

And so began one of my greatest life lessons.

"Easy wake-up?" he asked. "Have you thought of what it was like to wake, eat and freshen up? From your 20 spoons, give me however many you think appropriate." I meekly surrendered one. He smiled, saying, "Maybe on a good day that may be about right, but the day after a many-hour spinal surgery?" He took another of my spoons.

18 spoons left.

Chuck continued: "Your doctors and techs came in, poked, prodded, drew blood, had you roll over, sit up and tested leg strength, reflexes and sensory response. How hard or easy was this? I need some spoons." I surrendered one and he just stared at me then said, "OK, you can slide for now."

17 spoons left.

Chuck said the next real event was going to happen any minute, my first round of therapy for the day. Knowing the drill, I surrendered two more spoons, and with an ironic smile, Chuck smiled and reminded me that I could barely make it back into bed yesterday, and promptly confiscated two more.

13 spoons left.

He then asked what was happening the rest of the morning, after my therapy ended with him at 10 a.m. I was expecting visitors, and while I would be happy to see them, I knew they would zap my energy. Chuck took two spoons.

11 spoons left.

Chuck told me there would be more visits from the nurses, vitals, blood tests, and doctor, again. Chuck took two spoons.

Nine spoons left.

Lunch was my next, notable event. Although I knew I would barely eat because I would be exhausted, trusty Chuck took two spoons anyway.

Seven spoons left.

After lunch was another round of therapy, guaranteed to be more painful than the first morning round. He took five spoons. "Wait," I exclaimed, "I'm running out of spoons." Only two left and my timeline was only at 1:30 p.m.

Two spoons left.

Sighing knowingly, he said "Yes," as he took the last two spoons that were used to clean me up after therapy and more visitors.

No spoons by 3 p.m.

Still to come that day? Vitals and doctors' checkups. More visitors. Dinner. More visitors. Vitals, and on and on.

Chuck asked if I got the message. He asked me to look at my life and how I'd lived since the surgery nine months ago. Chuck was curious how many spoons I thought it took to walk and play golf carrying a 30-lb. golf bag in August. He asked if I did chores before or after golf. He talked about life-energy management, what I unrealistically expected from my body.

Chuck said I was there by choice, choices I'd made daily, using spoons I didn't have. He asked me if I liked him and I told him "Yes," and asked "Why?" His answer was direct, seemingly harsh at the time, but accurate: "Because I'll be seeing you again if you don't change. Next time you may not walk out of this hospital with the amount of damage you are inflicting on your body."

Chuck asked if I wanted to walk the golf course playing 18 holes or watch others play from a wheelchair.

While that was my third round of therapy with Chuck it was my eighth spinal surgery, each worse with more collateral damage, more nerve damage, more loss of strength and mobility. Upon reflection I had to acknowledge that my choices put me there.

I had to rethink my life. I don't play golf anymore; I can't. But I'm still walking and gratefully doing other fulfilling activities that were nearly lost to me.

About you

This lesson isn't only applicable to Bill or to people recovering from surgeries, folks with spinal cord injuries or other disabilities. It is a life lesson for every one of us.

Evaluate your daily life. How frequently are you using spoons you don't have?

Does this mean stop doing? Or does it mean look at yourself, what energy and physical health you have on any given day. Then look at what you'd like to do and or need to do and balance your choices. Some things don't have to be done today. Learn to say no when you're out of spoons.

While we've just looked at the physical ramifications of not practicing self-care, there are also emotional or thinking activities that wear you out. A rough business meeting could take four spoons; a call to a frustrated client, six.

Of course, there will always be days when we over-do it. But it's not about the one time you over-do it, it's about a lifestyle of over-doing.

No. 43 of 56 Ways

Have you guessed? That's right: get 20 plastic spoons. Walk through an easy day, average day, hard day. Be realistic. Everyone's morning wake-up routine takes a spoon – or two or three. Your commute, getting kids to school could take three more. Meetings, chores. If you're fair and honest, you'll likely find that typically five out of seven days you've used spoons you don't have. Learn to love yourself, honor your spoons, and use them wisely.

> **Meditation:** 19 to 20 minutes. You can do 20!

Day 44

MAKE STRESS YOUR FRIEND

Many people look to mindfulness to reduce the levels of stress in their life. Does this include you?

Early on we looked at the stress reaction, and how unchecked chronic stress is one of the biggest contributors to physical and mental illness. What if we told you there was another way to look at stress, another way to experience stress?

The University of Wisconsin-Madison conducted a study of 30,000 people asking this question:

Does the perception that stress affects health matter?

It was a significant and long-term study of a very large sample of people, and the results may come as a surprise.

Those experiencing high levels of stress who believed that stress was good for them:

    a.   Had the lowest mortality rates.

    b. Their blood vessels stayed open and healthy.

Highly stressed people who believed that stress was bad for their health:

    a. Had a higher chance of dying than those who looked at stress as a positive.
    b. Their blood vessels were constricted (as is seen in those with heart disease).

Conclusion: *Your beliefs about stress clearly affect how your health is impacted.* It's time to look a bit deeper and make stress your friend.

How to accomplish this is shockingly simple. Simply change the way you think about it – and that changes your body's response to it.

1. Next time you face a challenge and find your heart racing, breathing accelerating or body tensing *observe*.
2. Say *"thank you body"* for the stress response that is energizing your body.
    - Your faster heart rate is sending extra *oxygen* to your brain.
    - Your body is releasing adrenalin and other hormones.
    - This process is *sharpening your senses.*
    - And it is *boosting your immune system.*

By simply *observing* and *thanking* your body, making stress your friend, you:
- Are adding years to your life;
- Improving your productivity.

Our reality is shaped by both inside and outside events and thoughts. How we choose to interpret these events shapes our response.

Be mindful, observe without judgment

Pay attention in the present moment, embrace and explore your Triangle of Self-Awareness. When this becomes a habit – and this is a very good habit, one we should cultivate – we clearly see our thoughts, feelings, motivations and reactions. We pause and instead of reacting, we respond.

No. 44 of 56 Ways

Flip a switch, change a behavior while making stress your friend.

Situation	Thought	Feeling
I have a meeting.	I don't like this meeting.	Anger, anxiety, stress.

Behavior: You go to the meeting, but you're not happy. You might eat something comforting or bring along a snack to make you feel better. Now, you have a habit.

Something that makes you happy or brings comfort has distracted you from your feelings of anger and frustration about having to go to the meeting. Once it becomes a habit in this instance, it begins to become a habit in other areas of your life.

With mindfulness: You see the habit and now you can change it.

Situation	Thought	Feeling
I have a meeting.	I don't like this meeting, but I need to be there.	Calm, accepting.

Behavior: Before the meeting you might take a few deep breaths to calm yourself, a practice you will follow throughout the meeting if things get uncomfortable. You know that after the meeting you'll need a break, so plan to take a walk as a reward.

Taking breaths and a walk are long-term rewards. If they become habits, they are good ones. And with time, you will learn the difference between a *reward* and a *habit*. You have also changed your meeting experience from anger and stress to a positive stress response.

With mindfulness: You begin to understand the Triangle of Self-Awareness. You begin to recognize habits and understand that some nourish you in body, mind and spirit while others make you feel poorly and begin the negative voices to sound in your head. Now you can change your habit.

> **Meditation:** 19 to 20 minutes.

Day 45

ACCEPTANCE

Why is acceptance important?

In simplest terms, acceptance helps us work through difficult emotions. Acceptance is often hard, but when we accept things, our life becomes easier.

Co-author Bill Van Ollefen shared his story of pain in the introduction. He is often asked: How do you deal with this pain?

He admits that it is not easy, that it took years for him to accept his pain, but he is also quick to add that although his pain is much worse than it has ever been, his life has never been so blessed and lovely.

He has learned to accept his pain, to not push away his difficult emotions, and to meditate daily because it is in meditation that he has learned acceptance.

Most of us are not plagued by pain like Bill's. But every difficult emotion you have – because it is yours – can make you suffer.

What to do? Follow our three-prong approach!

1. **Allowing negative emotions to exist in your life — for the moment — does not mean that you've chosen to take no action.**

You are developing a different relationship to the experience – allowing it to happen and then letting it be.

You are aware of difficult feelings, register their presence, and then make a choice about how to respond. You are deliberately paying attention. You are not passive. And you are certainly not helpless.

2. **Denying that a negative thought or feeling is taking place is risky for your mental health.**

If you push negative thoughts, feelings or sensations aside that can become the first link in a mental chain that causes automatic, often critical habits to form.

Ever hear someone say: "I'm stupid to think like this" or "I should be strong enough to cope with that?"

Change the conversation. When you start thinking about negative or hurtful thoughts recognize that fear has intruded, and judgment is present. You are not denying. You are recognizing and facing the hard times.

3. **Acceptance helps you work through each unpleasant experience.**

We talk a lot about loving kindness and self-compassion. So again, let's talk about how to bring these traits into your life, using acceptance to deal with negative thoughts and emotions.

You can't will away the thoughts, nor can you will yourself to be compassionate and kind. So, you practice.

You use the Triangle of Self-Awareness. Daily. And often many times during the day. By using the triangle, when a difficult time arises, you will remember to notice how it is affecting your thoughts, emotions and body. For example, you might notice anxiety showing up as a tightness in your chest or sadness making your tummy ache or your shoulders sag.

We have spoken before about how an inquisitive mind can help you understand what is happening in your body. When you are distressed, this is the perfect opportunity to explore. Curiosity is a luxury most of us often don't offer ourselves.

And the more you practice this, the more you begin to realize that you can allow unpleasant experiences in, accept them, and still be OK.

No. 45 of 56 Ways

Throughout the day, as soon as your heart begins to race or your forehead and shoulders start tensing, take five deep breaths. Poll your Triangle of Self-Awareness.

> **Meditation:** 19 to 20 minutes.

Day 46

IMPERMANENCE

They say that there are only two things you can be sure of: death and taxes. We add change to that list. Back in the early '70s, David Bowie brought the word to the forefront – "ch-ch-ch-ch-changes" – and for many, that is how they approach change, by singing it away or stumbling through the experience.

Here are two ways of looking at impermanence:

> *"That nothing is static or fixed, that all is fleeting and impermanent, is the first mark of existence."*
> —Pema Chödron,
> an American Tibetan Buddhist

> *"No man ever steps in the same river twice, for it's not the same river and he's not the same man."*
> —HERACLITUS,
> PRE-SOCRATIC IONIAN GREEK PHILOSOPHER

Teaching impermanence to our clients is one of our favorite topics. We have found it is something that people don't think about often and hardly ever talk about, even though we face it every day of our lives. It's become that proverbially background noise we ignore.

When you are facing something you dislike doing or makes you uncomfortable, how wonderful is it to think that this will eventually end? Unfortunately, many of us tend to concentrate on the event, welcoming stress into our bodies, never considering that the event is impermanent and will pass.

Of course, there are so many glorious things that come into your life, and although you would love to make each permanent, in most cases they will leave your world.

We prescribe to the words of the Buddhist monk Thich Nhat Hahn: "It is not impermanence that makes you suffer. What makes you suffer is wanting things to be permanent when they are not."

Enter stress

Unfortunately, be the change good or bad, it often comes with a component of stress. Adapting to change is usually hard.

Just think about the normal consequences of life: aging, sickness, death. And what about emotions: joy, sadness, happiness?

The big but

Thanks to impermanence, everything is possible. If you begin to accept impermanence as part of your life and view it not as a threat, you begin the path to coping with, and then embracing, change.

Consider this: Are you the same person that you were 46 days ago, when you first picked up this book? If you are doing the daily exercises and meditating, you are now realizing that you are not. You are shifting, evolving and growing.

Some examples:
- If you are in good health and are aware of impermanence, you will take good care of yourself, live each day with present-moment awareness, and enjoy your being.
- When you know that the person you love is impermanent, you will cherish your beloved all the more.
- When you are facing a move, you know the packing and unpacking will eventually end, and you can enjoy the experience.

Impermanence teaches you to respect and value every moment and all the precious things around you and inside of you. When you practice the mindfulness of impermanence, you become fresher and more loving.

Once you recognize that all things are impermanent, you have no problem enjoying them. Real peace and joy are only possible when you see clearly into the nature of impermanence.

Awareness of impermanence and appreciation of your human potential will give you a sense of urgency that you must use every precious moment in your life, embracing the good with the bad.

No. 46 of 56 Ways

Today, take note of something in your life that is impermanent. Write down what it is. Is this a good or bad change? Poll your Triangle of

Self-Awareness. How is it affecting your thoughts, emotions and physical sensations? Can you accept this change as a part of your life? Bring it into present-moment awareness, and embrace every aspect of the event.

> **Meditation**: 19 to 20 minutes. Come on – you can do 20!

Day 47

EQUANIMITY

Have you ever met someone so well grounded that no matter what happens to them, they have an uncanny ability to somehow just be OK with it?

They are practicing equanimity and you are well on your way to being able to attain this ability. You've come a long way, exploring many topics on the path to mindfulness, including the workings and interactions of your mind, emotions and physical self.

Your meditation practice is helping you reshape your brain, mind and patterns of behavior. You are learning awareness with loving kindness and self-compassion without judgment.

Combined they enable you to exist in a state of equanimity.

Equanimity defined

Let's start with these two concepts:
- The steadiness of your mind under stress.
- Developing a sense of inner balance.

Here's an even better one:
- *The ability to accept life as it comes to you without blaming anything or anyone.*

Think of equanimity as the ease that comes from seeing with understanding, or to see with patience, remaining centered in the middle of whatever is happening.

You see without being caught by what you see, aware without entanglement

You may ask, isn't this the same as indifference? Not even close. In fact, indifference is the near opposite of equanimity, deceptively similar but very different.

Equanimity includes a *sense of care and attentiveness* to your life – rather than indifference – plus loving-kindness, compassion, sympathetic joy.

Why do we want equanimity?

With equanimity:
- You are not caught up in your ego;
- You can experience pleasant and unpleasant events with equal attention;
- You notice and care – even deeply – about what is going on;
- Instead of reacting to your thoughts or feelings, you respond mindfully.

Or, in the words of an American monk, Bhikkhu Bodhi: "It is evenness of mind, unshakeable freedom of mind, a state of inner balance that cannot be upset by gain or loss, dishonor or praise, pleasure or pain."

Having equanimity does not mean suppressing emotions or giving up your impressions of your life experiences. You want to feel joy and you welcome it because it involves pleasure. It can also be appropriate to feel sad, such as when grieving the loss of a loved one.

What do we need to develop equanimity?

1. **A trained mind.** You've been working on this for quite some time now. You have learned to observe your thoughts without judgment, focus on some while dismissing unwanted or distracting thoughts.
2. **Mental calmness.** The physical changes in the brain along with your lessons teach you to respond rather than react.
3. **Integrity, authenticity, confidence.** These parts of yourself allow you to fully engage with life and interface with the outside world as well as your mind.
4. **Understanding of impermanence.** It's not difficult to see the value of both impermanence and equanimity. You can engage with the unpleasant knowing it will end or change. The realization that things change also encourages you to really embrace, engage and linger with pleasant events when presented to you.
5. **Even temper even in difficult situations.** Every meditation, every lesson learned changes you, helps you develop your mind and understand your behavior. The whole process teaches you to pause, observe and respond, preventing runaway or unskillful emotions and reactions.

Reflections: Pen/pencil time!

> *"We practice equanimity by contemplating how all beings are similar to ourselves in that they, too, wish to gain happiness and be free of suffering, regardless of whether we would consider them our friends, enemies, or strangers."*
> —DALAI LAMA

Reflect on the benefit of a mind that has balance and equanimity. Sense what a gift it can be to bring a peaceful heart to the world around you. What can you do to bring balance and equanimity to your world?

_____
_____
_____

How will you feel this inner sense of balance and ease?

_____
_____
_____

Equanimity meditation

The following meditation is on www.PathwayToMindfulness.com, Meditation tab, scroll down to Audio Meditations titled Equanimity. It's adapted from a meditation by Jack Kornfield, author and teacher.

May I be balanced and at peace.

All created things arise and pass away: joys, sorrows, pleasant events, people, buildings, animals, nations, even whole civilizations. Let yourself rest in the midst of them.

May I see the rising and passing of all nature with equanimity and balance. May I be open and balanced and peaceful.

Acknowledge that all beings have their own path – that their lives rise and pass away.

May I bring compassion and equanimity to the events of the world. May I find balance and equanimity and peace.

No. 47 of 56 Ways

Instead of watching TV today, speak with someone you live with or call a friend. As you are talking, ask yourself, "Am I in equanimity?" If not, ask, "How can I achieve equanimity?"

> **Meditation:** 20 minutes. You did it!

Day 48

GRATITUDE

ARE YOU GRATEFUL? IF so, good for you, because research studies have proven that grateful people are:
- Happier;
- Have better relationships than those who are ungrateful;
- Have improved work performance.

None of this should come as a surprise because gratitude is an affirmation of goodness – that there are good things in the world and there are gifts and benefits to being grateful.

Gratitude reaps even more benefits for those who understand that this goodness is outside themselves. They acknowledge that other people, or a higher power if they so believe, give us gifts, both big and small, which bring goodness into our lives.

Added gratitude benefits

1. **Better sleep.**

Let's start with what happens when you don't sleep well:
- poor job satisfaction;
- poor executive functioning;
- less innovative thinking, lower occupational performance, more safety errors and work injuries.

Sleep deprivation also negatively affects relationships. Sleep-deprived people are less trusting of others and more impatient, frustrated and hostile. Negative, critical thoughts tend to induce sleeplessness. Sleep is the mind and body's quintessential restorative activity.

Grateful thinking and grateful moods help you sleep better and longer. In one study, people who kept a gratitude journal slept on average 30 minutes more per night, woke up feeling more refreshed, and had an easier time staying awake during the day compared to those who didn't practice gratitude.

The National Sleep Foundation says that 95 percent of the population need seven-to-eight hours of sleep a night. Unfortunately, 30 percent of us are logging fewer than six hours. Why is this important?

The NSF says that sleep is essential for good health, mental and emotional functioning and safety, while The Rand Corporation determines that sleep deprivation costs U.S. companies more than $400 billion in lost productivity.

2. **Reduced excessive entitlement.**

People with excessive entitlement engage in counterproductive behaviors and actions designed to harm an organization or its members: theft, aggression, violence, sabotage, withdrawal, deliberate poor performance, and threatening, abusing and blaming others.

Entitlement can also show up as gossip, complaining and negativity – and that can affect relationships. A person who is entitled to everything is grateful for nothing. Gratitude therefore is the antidote to entitlement.

People who are grateful are 20-to-30 percent less likely to be annoyed, irritated and aggressive. They are also less susceptible to having their feelings hurt, and, when their feelings are hurt, they are less likely to strike back.

3. **Makes us better employees.**

Research has shown that gratitude is a driver of "pro-social" (kind and helpful) behavior and makes better organizational citizens. These employees are more likely to:
- Volunteer for extra work assignments;
- Take time to mentor coworkers;
- Be compassionate when someone has a problem;
- Encourage and praise others.

And who doesn't love working with people like this!

Grateful people are more creative, innovative, flexible, open, curious and love learning. A recent study showed that love of learning and gratitude were the strongest predictors of overall well-being.

No. 48 of 56 Ways

You're journaling, right? Now we have something for you to add to your journal nightly: Make a list of everything you were grateful for today. They can be little or huge events. Just the act of writing down your grateful thoughts will set you up for a better night's sleep – at least 30 more minutes of sleep than you would have logged if you didn't keep the journal. At the end of the week, if you do this nightly, that's 3.5 hours each week.

> **Meditation:** 20 minutes!

Day 49

REVIEW

If you learned anything this week, we hope you take the lesson of the 20 spoons to heart.

After years of teaching mindfulness, this is the lesson that all of our long-term clients think about daily. When they use all their spoons – and let's face it, many of us do daily – they start practicing the other lessons we touched on this week:
- They learn to make stress their friend, because when you use all your spoons, stress will begin to rear its ugly head;
- They embrace acceptance, accepting that this is how their life is right now, and that leads to the next lesson, welcoming impermanence.
- They develop equanimity to be present in the moment, aware without entanglement.
- And finally, they keep their gratitude journal because they know that sleep has the ability to heal, and the gratitude journal will positively influence their sleep.

The 20 spoons teach many lessons, but perhaps the most critical is that you can't do it all, nor should you try. It also teaches you to evaluate your daily life so before you say "yes" to something, you might consider how to say "no."

Reflections: Go back and re-read your contract. Commit again.

No. 49 on 56 Ways

Ask a friend, relative or work colleague about what they do in their free time. Really listen to their responses.

> **Meditation:** 20 and holding! If the time seems long, go back to the beginning and review the anchors – breath, visualization, counting.

Week 8

Your thought for the week:

Don't trade authenticity for approval.

Day 50

AUTHENTICITY

Authenticity is one of the most important, but also most challenging ingredients in creating healthy and sustainable relationships.

Why? *Fear.* If we truly show ourselves, we fear what others might think.

We spend our lives saying, doing, acting, feeling in ways that others will accept.

What is authenticity?

Authenticity is the daily practice of letting go of who we are supposed to be and embracing who we actually are.

So how do you become authentic?

- First, you have to understand – and believe – that you don't have to be liked by everyone, which is an impossible goal.

- You embrace loving kindness and self-compassion, which is all about respect for self.
- You are willing to show your true self, warts and all. What is the worst that can happen? Someone might not like something about you?

Let's flip this a bit and ask: What is the worst thing about not showing your true self? It is the damage you are doing to you, since you are only showing a part of yourself and locking away the rest –

and that is exhausting.

Now think about someone you know and like. Aren't their warts and peculiarities part of their charm?

Through meditation you lean in. You listen to what is true in your heart, listen to what you need. And sometimes that involves change.

The most successful change comes from a base of loving kindness. Authenticity. Self-Compassion.

Game plan

- Weekly, make a three-category priority list: silos for work, relationships, self. And refer to this daily.
- The three silos are important. If you forget slotting in time for relationships and self, they might never happen. Without caring for self and your relationships, your life is not complete.
- And by including the last two silos, you are honoring your authentic self.

Reflections: Pen/pencil time!

Think about a recent experience you had with a friend, family member, co-worker, client, where you wanted to be authentic but could not find the right words.

What was it?
___
___
___

And now ask yourself the following questions. Some you might be able to answer right now. Others may take some time:

1. What was I afraid would happen if I shared my experience with this person?
___
___
___

2. How do I feel knowing I did not share what I was thinking and feeling?
___
___
___

3. If I weren't afraid, what would I most want to say to this person right now?
___
___
___

4. How can I share this the next time I am with this person?
___
___
___

5. Do I become a different person depending on my surroundings or the people I am with?
_____
_____
_____

6. Do I worry that people will not like the real me so I show up as the person I think they will like?
_____
_____
_____

Going forward

Try these four techniques to help you through any difficult, uncomfortable or new situations:

1. **Be earnestly self-aware:** Begin by observing yourself when you meet new people, in social and work settings, and with loved ones and friends. Notice how you feel in each situation.

When am I most comfortable?
_____
_____
_____

When am I least comfortable?
_____
_____
_____

Poll your thoughts, emotions and physical sensations. When you understand why and how situations affect you, then you can intentionally bring your authentic self.

2. **Find real connections:** Begin to really get to know the people in your life – be it a family member or a co-worker you recently met. Ask them questions, and most importantly, listen to the answers. There is a strong connection that comes with listening intently. As you get to know this person better, you will be developing a more authentic relationship, which allows you to show your true self.

3. **Shed perfection:** This is a common thread throughout our book, but it is so important because too many of us demand perfection – in ourselves and others. Repeat after us: Perfection is impossible. Make it a life goal, to accept imperfection. Embrace your imperfections, and the imperfections of others. Your imperfections are what make you unique and interesting. Plus, dare to be a bit vulnerable.

4. **Be present:** Have you ever been in the middle of a conversation with someone and your mind begins to wander? You think the person who is talking has no idea your mind has wandered, but most people intuitively sense another person's focus and attention – and that can stop any conversation. Be present in every conversation. Give people your full attention. Mastering the art of presence is a sure way to ensure authenticity.

5. **Practice self-care:** Sleep more? Exercise? Eat healthy? Lose weight? Gain weight? Meditate daily? Take a bath to calm a frazzled day? New haircut? New clothes? It's up to you.

The path to authenticity: More pen/pencil time!

What would make me feel better about me?
_____
_____
_____

What is my action plan for making me feel better about me?
___
___
___

Think of a time when I talked about something that required action but there was no action. What could I have done differently?
___
___
___

Think of a time when I had an *I can't* attitude. What could I have done differently to replace the *I can't* with an *I can*?
___
___
___

Think of a time when I took the easy way out. What could I have done differently to make the experience more meaningful?
___
___
___

Think of a time I blamed someone else for something I did. What could I have done differently?
___
___
___

Your sense of self-worth is defined by how you live your life, regardless of your socio-economic position. Can you look yourself in the mirror at the end of the day and honestly say "I've done my best. I have been my authentic self throughout the day."

No. 50 of 56 Ways

Three times during the day, do 10 backward and 10 forward shoulder rolls. Pay attention to these movements. How do they make you feel? Are you engaging any other parts of your body?

> **Meditation:** Forever 20 minutes!

Day 51

CAN YOU JUDGE?

MINDFULNESS IS ALL ABOUT AWARENESS. Without judgment. Or at least that's what we told you in the beginning of the book.

But can we judge? Maybe a better question would be: Is it possible not to judge?

We can and will judge. Judgments may come from our innate moral compass. For example, how do you not judge someone whose actions or behaviors transgress your most basic values? Extremely difficult. How about the thief, abuser, murderer or bully?

A parent might judge their child's behavior as inappropriate or dangerous and set boundaries. Not only is this reasonable, it is responsible and part of their obligations as a parent.

Let's look at more common types of judgment.

One example could be food, some particular item, dish, recipe or cuisine. Our mind asks: "Does it taste good?" Depending on what it is, we judge the food.

Your mind automatically judges things as good or bad, right or wrong, fair or unfair. This happens so fast you are not aware of the judging, and your experiences are then automatically colored and shaped as you become aware of them. But mindfulness is about being aware of that part of you and taking a fresh perspective.

The key here is to bring awareness and intentionality to the moments of your life.

Be aware when your brain is automatically judging a situation or a person. Pause and develop some perspective.

Was this judgment just something that popped into your mind? Is it something that should be judged? Are you judging your own or someone else's emotions, feelings, observations?

Bring on the food

Is there another way to look at this?

Let's go back to food. Have you ever heard someone say a particular cuisine is bad?

Let's use Indian food. When recently making dinner plans with friends an Indian restaurant was suggested, and someone said, "Indian food is bad, horrible." And yet, reservations are difficult to come by at that restaurant. Why? Because the food is *not* bad or horrible, and those that love Indian food, find this particular restaurant serves the best in the area.

A better way to say something might be: "I don't care for Indian cuisine." Or better yet, "I went to that particular restaurant and didn't care for the food."

Do you see the distinction? We are talking about a preference that should not be a pronouncement of fact.

Mindfulness is about being alive. It brings back the choice and wonder available to you in everyday life. In the above situation you may look at a menu and see tandoori chicken, a marvelous meal that you might be willing to try. Plus, if you keep an open mind, you may discover you really like this different and tasty dish.

Let's look at a situation with several components and ways to assess, judge and see how it affects us.

Situation: You're driving down a busy highway and someone passes you driving 40mph over the limit, weaving through traffic.

Thought: That driver is crazy, an idiot, a bad driver.

Observation and description: I am startled and have a stress reaction. I get angry. My blood pressure goes up, heart beats faster, my entire body is upset. I may also then internalize it, saying "Why did he do this to me?" That further fuels the reaction. These are physically and emotionally uncomfortable feelings.

Nonjudgmental assessment: Take a breath. Yikes, that person is driving dangerously. This is an observation of facts. The breath helps ratchet down a runaway reaction and leaves room to replace it with a measured response. I am safe.

Add curiosity. I wonder why he did that? Perhaps he had a critically ill child in the back seat that you may not have noticed. Or…. fill in the blank with another possible and valid reason.

Possible results

- You circumvented a full-stress cycle that would upset your body for an hour or so and yes, ruin your trip;
- By reevaluating the situation, not judging the driver, you make a factual observation about the driving behavior. Any thought that this is a valid emergency could bring a measure of compassion

and stop the negative personalization of the event, even if it is not the truth!
- The best outcome: This will be a fleeting moment in your day, neither over- nor under-influencing your thoughts, feelings and physical sensations.

No. 51 of 56 Ways

At the end of the day, reflect on the day and notice how frequently you make judgments, pronouncements – both out loud or in your own mind. This means that today you will have to notice what is going on. If you are reading this at night, do the exercise tomorrow.

Notice how your judgments subtly or dramatically shaped and colored the experiences. Notice how your body was affected.

Determine a more skillful or mindful way to assess situations and events less judgmentally, and what the outcome and results might have been.

> **Meditation:** 20 minutes. Aren't you proud of *you*?

Day 52

AWE AND WONDER

Just watch a baby lying in his crib, looking all around at the sights and sounds. Sometimes babies stare. Often, they react, squealing, smiling, crying. They are on a journey of discovery, and this new world of theirs is filled with awe and wonder. Everything is magical, bigger than life.

When was the last time you were immersed in awe and wonder, amazed or fascinated by an encounter that is beyond your ordinary framework of understanding?

When feeling awe, you may feel small, insignificant, and yet connected with the world around you, in touch with something greater than yourself. Time seems to expand as you absorb the present moment, detached from your normal, mundane concerns.

Why should you seek awe? A study from the University of California, Berkeley, suggests that the feeling of awe you may experience during encounters with art, nature and spirituality has an anti-inflammatory effect, protecting the body from chronic disease.

Who doesn't want some of that?

The researchers found a correlation between feelings of awe and lower levels of cytokines, markers that put the immune system on high alert by triggering a defensive reaction known as inflammation. While inflammation is essential to fighting infection and disease when the body is presented with a specific threat, chronically high levels of cytokines have been linked to health problems, including heart disease, Alzheimer's, depression and autoimmune conditions.

In awe you find balance and renew your connection to self, your inner truths, and your authentic self.

And guess what?

Mindfulness is a key element in bringing awe into your daily life.

Once you begin thinking about awe and seeking it out, you begin to realize how omnipresent it is in life. You become child-like, moving through your day and noticing the moments of wonder that normally go unnoticed.

These are not life-changing events. Perhaps you can watch two squirrels at play. Or go into the grocery store and really look at the beauty of flowers, the different parts of each and the colors that make up the whole. Get up early and watch the sunrise. Or be sure to catch the sun as it sets each night.

Nothing monumental here, simply ordinary, until you gaze with wonder. Then they take on a new life, and you begin to reap the benefits – lower levels of our new friend, cytokines.

Go out and find your awe moments. Listen to them carefully. See where they guide you. They all can stir up humility and wonder. They will also bring a new appreciation for what is all around. Maybe you'll attend more concerts, visit museums or take a hike in the woods, always a breeding ground for wonder.

We promise it is there. You merely have to seek it out.

Reflections: Pen/pencil time!

Think of the places in your home where you can seek awe. A painting or picture hanging on your wall? A scene out a window? An inspiring piece of music? Think hard. It's there. You just need to find it. Did you?
_____
_____

Is there a daytrip you can take – in nature, a museum, aquarium, to an amazing restaurant – that will spark awe? What is it and when will you go?
_____
_____
_____

Look at this week's weather forecast. Is there a day that will be sunny and clear? Get up early and watch the sun rise. Write down your plan.
_____
_____
_____

Tonight, try to catch the sun set. You don't even have to physically watch the sun as it slips out of sight. You can simply sit in your home and watch the day's colors change until night descends. It's a wonderful way to say good-bye to the day.
_____
_____
_____

No. 52 of 56 Ways

Eat a meal today in silence. No talk. No TV. No music. Just you and your food. Savor every bite. Look at the food and think about how it arrived on your plate. That trip alone can bring about a feeling of awe, since each ingredient probably traveled so far to reach you. If you grew it yourself, all the better. The many steps it took to grow from seed to your plate is wondrous, the gift of life.

> **Meditation:** 20 minutes of unguided insight meditation.

What follows is one of our favorite ways to bring awe and wonder into your life – without leaving your house. The meditation is at www.PathwayToMindfulness.com, Meditation tab, scroll down to Audio Meditations, titled Awe and wonder.

Awe and Wonder meditation

In life it is so tempting to measure and compare….
Something
Someone
Some where
Some time.

When we measure, we come up short not seeing the whole.
Breathe, settle.

Now turn inward. See yourself.

Be in awe at the very process of life unfolding in you continually.

Each breath oxygenating the blood…more than 23,000 times each day.

Each heartbeat sending nourishing blood coursing through your hungry body…more than 115,000 times each day.

Your brain, trillions of nerve synapses…firing more than 100 trillion times each day…more than 70,000 thoughts each day.

Who am I?

What am I?

What am I feeling?

Expand your awareness to where you are, right here. Right now….

With your eyes closed, imagine the wonder at the movement all around you.

And now wonder at the ever-changing stillness.

Notice the light streaming through the shadow of your eyes.

No evaluation, no comparison, simply awe…and wonder.

In your mind's eye stand, filled with wonder, at the edge of a meadow in the bright warm sun….

The meadow is filled with wildflowers of every type, every color in the rainbow, as far as you can see. Notice the fragrance of the flowers carried on a soft warm breeze.

Look down at your feet. See the infinite simplicity and complexity of the spider's web catching and reflecting the sunlight.

Who am I?

What am I?

What am I feeling?

Find yourself at the ocean's edge…

What do you see?

Imagine what you can't see below the surface, beyond your gaze.

What do you hear and smell? Be in awe of the vastness of the great body of water, drawing your thoughts, taking you away from self.

Who am I?

What am I?

What am I feeling?

Where am I?

Now find yourself in a dark meadow on a cloudless night. Gaze in awe at the night sky, stars, galaxies, now lost in the infinite....

Who am I?

What am I?

What am I feeling?

Where do I fit?

What is my purpose?

In awe we seek to find our place. We reorient ourselves to us and the world around.

Day 53

HOW TO SAY *"NO"*

How many times have you said *yes* when you really meant *no*? If you're like most of us, the answer is probably waaaayyyyyyy too often.

As soon as the *yes* is uttered, you are already beating yourself up, maybe getting your critical inner voice jabbering away, and that one *yes* could ruin even the nicest day.

Making the case to say *no*

First, you need to tell yourself that it's impossible to do everything. Perhaps you said *yes* to too many things that are now consuming your time. Or maybe you just want more time for yourself, which is a commitment, one that takes time, and you need to recognize this. The latter is so important for authenticity and self-care. Remember the spoons.

Next, you need to understand that saying *no* does not mean you are selfish. Many people say *yes* because a *no* would make them feel guilty or they feel they are letting people down who need their help. Consider this: If you are truly selfish, you would not feel guilty. Ever!

It's impossible to please everyone: You just must believe this. Acknowledging that it's impossible to please every person in your life and that you should draw the line somewhere can be so freeing. Also, if you say *yes* to everything, then people will be more likely to take advantage of you and to ask you to do too many favors.

When you say *no*, think of everything you are saying *yes* to. Saying *no* is often not a negative. If you're saying *no* to doing more work, you're saying *yes* to a variety of things that will benefit your life. Make a list of what you are saying *yes* to in your life.

How do you say *no*?

1. Be honest.
2. Don't over-explain.
3. Do give a reason why but keep it brief.

The script

Just say, "I'm sorry. I can't do this right now." Use a sympathetic but firm tone. If pressured as to why, reply that it doesn't fit with your schedule, and change the subject. Most reasonable people will accept this as an answer, so if someone keeps pressuring you, they're being rude, and it's OK to just repeat, "I'm sorry, but this just doesn't fit with my schedule," and change the subject, or even walk away if you have to.

Give yourself time. If you're uncomfortable being firm or dealing with pushy people, it's OK to say, "Let me think about it and get back to you." This gives you a chance to review your schedule, as well as your feelings about saying *yes* to another commitment. Do a cost-benefit analysis, and then get back to them with a *yes* or *no*. Most importantly: It helps you avoid letting yourself be pressured into overscheduling your life and taking on too much stress.

Say *yes* to something else: If you would really like to do what they're requesting, but don't have the time (or are having trouble accepting that you don't), it's fine to say, "I can't do this, but I *can*…" and mention a lesser commitment that you can make. This way you'll still be partially involved, but it will be on your own terms.

Last thoughts

1. **Be firm** – not defensive or overly apologetic – and polite. This gives the signal that you are sympathetic but will not easily change your mind if pressured.
2. **Be clear.** If you decide to tell the person you'll get back to them, be matter of fact and not too promising. If you lead people to believe you'll likely say *yes* later, they'll be more disappointed with a later *no*.
3. **No excuses necessary.** If asked for an explanation, remember that you really don't owe one. "It doesn't fit with my schedule," is perfectly acceptable.
4. **Prioritize.** Remember that there are only so many hours in the day. This means that whatever you choose to take on limits your ability to do other things. Even if you somehow could fit a new commitment into your schedule, if it's not more important than what you would have to give up to do it – including time for meditation, relaxation and self-care – you really don't have the time in your schedule

Reflections: Pen/pencil time!

1. Think of a time when I said *yes* and I should have said *no*.
___
___
___

2. If I had said *no*, how would that have helped my life?
   _____
   _____
   _____

3. What are some ways that will help me say *no* in the future?
   _____
   _____
   _____

4. Define my life's purpose.
   - What is my life's purpose? If it is razor sharp, the *how* is easy. Define my purpose:
     _____
     _____
     _____

   - We only have one pass at this life – so live it the way you want not the way other people want you to live.
   - Say *yes* to anything that helps you achieve your life's purpose.

5. Focus on what really matters.
   - Focus is critical – and hard to sustain. It's easy to lose clarity.
   - Having focus is critical, but it's never easy.
   - Say *no* to what's not critical so you can say *yes* to your life's purpose. How best can I focus on my passion?
     _____
     _____
     _____

6. Dig deep.
   - It is impossible to be good at everything.
   - Dive deep inside to find your passions.
   - Consider this: When you don't know what to say *no* to, it's hard to know when you should say *yes*.

- What are my passions, which should align with my purpose?
  _____
  _____
  _____

7. Speak with conviction.
   - "A no uttered from deepest conviction is better than a yes merely uttered to please, or worse, to avoid trouble."—*Mahatma Gandhi*
   - Saying *no* is a decision.
   - If you learn to say *no* with conviction, this will help you to say *yes* with conviction to the things that help you reach your purpose.

8. It comes down to you.
   - "When you say *yes* to others, make sure you are not saying *no* to yourself."— *author Paulo Coelho*

No. 53 of 56

Make a list of everything you must do today. Next to each item write a *yes* or *no* – meaning it's something you should have said *yes* to, or something that does not fit in with your life's purpose and you should have said *no*. If possible, do this for a week so you can really see how you have organized your life.

> **Meditation:** 20 minutes of unguided mindful meditation.

Day 54

EXPECTATIONS

Daily – at work, at home, on vacation – no matter where you go or what you do, you deal with expectations. Sometimes they are yours, sometimes they are the expectations of the people around you.

Cleary defined expectations are beliefs about the way something will happen in the future. An outcome, a result.

Unfortunately, you become attached to expectations. While that sounds normal enough have you ever thought about the downside of having expectations? There are consequences when you become attached to your expectations.

What happens when your expectations are not met? The easiest consequence to recognize is the emotional impact.

Sometimes the emotion is as simple as disappointment. However, it could easily be frustration or even anger. What does this do to your mind and body? How does it shape and color the entire experience?

Here's an example. Suppose you're going on a summer vacation to the beach and the day you arrive it's raining and there is a hurricane warning posted for later in the week. How do you react emotionally? It probably won't be a warm, happy response. Would this ruin the day or week?

Suppose you're going to a favorite restaurant and know exactly what you're planning to order. Maybe they make the best meatloaf you've ever had. In fact, you've been tasting it in your mind's eye all day. So yummy. And then the waiter dashes your expectations saying they're out of meatloaf for the day. No warm, happy feelings here.

Dr. Lo, one of co-author Bill Van Ollefen's early meditation teachers, saw he was frustrated one day and inquired why. Bill told his tale of woe, of plans long in the making gone awry and expectations dashed.

Dr. Lo listened attentively, smiled and said, "Who has no expectations is rarely disappointed." Bill thought about it and although he understood what he meant, he thought it was unrealistic, almost dumb, not to have expectations and outcomes to look forward to. He thought it would take away the excitement and anticipation, which he told Dr. Lo. His response, which at the time added to Bill's confusion: "Life is a is a journey, not a destination."

This was entirely too complicated for Bill's adolescent brain, so he asked for more help, more clarification.

Dr. Lo said the lesson is twofold. The first is quite clear: The greater your expectations, the more attached you become to a specific outcome, the worse you feel when it isn't met.

However, he continued, asking, "What opportunities have you missed or lost focused on and attached to the outcome?"

Consider the rainy beach day spent pouting versus visiting a local attraction. The latter result might be more memorable, which often happens with an unexpected adventure on the vacation. As for the hurricane warning: That is for later in the week, the course could veer in another direction, and worrying about it until it is real is useless.

What do you think about the restaurant experience? Pouting and putting yourself into a totally negative mindset could ruin the rest of the meal. If you free yourself of disappointment, recognizing that a whole menu of delights await, dinner becomes a journey not a meatloaf destination.

Can you see how this frees you?

Things to think about:

1. **Set healthy expectations.**
    a. For yourself and others.
    b. Make sure expectations are reasonable.

2. **Be willing to shift**
    a. Things change. Often an unexpected circumstance comes along to shift the planned experience and outcome.
    b. Poll your Triangle of Self-Awareness to discover how you are feeling – thoughts, emotions, physical sensations. This lets you pause and take some breaths.
    c. Don't immediately pivot in another direction. Think it through.
    d. If there are others involved, talk about what is happening. Communication becomes the anchor to solve the issue. Then either you alone or together with others – depending on the situation – decide what happens next.
    e. You have consciously noted your feelings and are managing your expectations in a thoughtful, carefully planned manner.

No. 54 of 56 Ways

Think of an expectation that, though unmet, opened you to a wonderful or special event.

Now think of a current expectation and see if you are too attached to the outcome. Think about how the whole journey can become the focal point.

Meditation: 20 minutes

Day 55

CURIOSITY

We think of mindfulness and curiosity as BFFs.

Think of mindfulness as the friend who quietly observes new things, while curiosity digs deeper and explores, looking at all the details and willing to play with each new finding.

Curiosity is an important part of awareness and insight. It keeps you from:
- Over-thinking;
- Focusing on a particular point;
- Looking for a specific answer.

Curiosity is your guide, leading you to mindful investigation and exploration, and that ultimately helps you to fully understand your experiences as they are. You learn to stay with whatever is happening – whether it is wanted or unwanted – and begin to allow and accept. It also expands your capacity for compassion.

Ponder this:
- Millions saw the apple fall. But Newton asked why?

- "The important thing is not to stop questioning. Curiosity has its own reason for existing." – *Albert Einstein*
- "Curiosity leads us to mindful investigation and exploration, helps us to fully know our experiences as they are, staying with whatever is happening. We keep moving forward, opening new doors and doing new things, because we're curious and curiosity keeps leading us down new paths." – *Walt Disney*

The Four Stages of Mindfulness

With only a day left in this journey, it's a great time to look at the stages of mindfulness and try to picture where you are now in this journey.

Based on neuroscientist Rick Hanson's writings, these four stages help us understand our journey to a mindful life. In psychology, these four stages correlate to the Hierarchy of Competence.

Know that these stages are not linear. You may straddle two stages. Or, on a Monday you may be at Stage 4, and Tuesday you are in crisis, and you find yourself back a stage, maybe even two. But here's the beauty of this journey, if you continue to meditate daily: When you find yourself back at Stage 2 or Stage 3, you will be more resilient, and before long, you are mindfully aware in the present moment.

Stage 1: Unaware (Unconsciously Incompetent)
- Stuck in all your normal patterns.
- Constantly shifting between feeling in control and out of control.
- Focus is a jumble of present, past and future, compromising the present.
- Blaming yourself and feeling hopeless.
- You focus on your problems.

Mindfulness may sound too good to be true or not possible for you.

Stage 2: Uncertain (Consciously Incompetent)
- Initial awareness of mindfulness through recognizing your wandering mind during meditation.
- Beginning to use your new skills.
- Seeing the possibility of mindfulness but afraid it won't work for you.
- Beginning to understand yourself and cautiously hopeful.
- Struggling with your old habits that pull you back into the familiar, your comfort zone.

Don't give up too soon or you can regress.

Stage 3: Aware (Consciously Competent)
- The old "normal" is broken.
- Feelings of loss of control are infrequent and shorter.
- Mindfulness is slowly becoming the more natural state and preferred.
- You feel like you are in charge and finally free.
- Your energy is focused on practicing self-care.

Mindfulness takes time. Remain non-judgmental and develop curiosity about life.

Stage 4: Natural (Unconsciously Competent)
- Mindfulness has become a part of your daily life, at home at work, out and about.
- You effortlessly embrace practicing present-moment awareness.
- You are confident and in control, no runaway reactions.
- You are energetic and living a more vibrant life.

Mindfulness has become a part of your daily life, home, work, relationships.

Reflections: Pen/pencil time!

Think of something that made you curious, something you really wanted to find out more about.

Now write down all the new things you learned because you were curious.

No. 55 of 56 Ways

Find something in your home that you've forgotten you have. Look at it with fresh eyes. Ask yourself: What is it? Why did I buy it? If it was given to you, who was the giver? If mechanical, how does it work? What is it?

You get the idea. Really look at this item and find out as much about it as you can. Now ask: What did I learn?

Meditation: 20 minutes!

Day 56

YOU MADE IT!

We hope you enjoyed this journey as much as we enjoyed leading you.

Since we began Pathway to Mindfulness, our goal has been to change the lives of our clients, one person at a time. In most cases we work as a pair, and there really are not enough hours in the day, days in the week, for us to reach as many people as we want.

Enter this book.

We truly believe that if everyone immersed themselves in mindfulness, meditated daily, and paid attention to the little things in life that can bring so much happiness, our world would be a better place.

Imagine holiday dinners if each of your friends and relatives embraced mindfulness. Can you? Everyone would be impeccable with their words, would really listen to what others were saying, be kinder, gentler and more authentic, and be able to accept the faults of others because they have learned that perfection is unattainable.

Our hope is that this book has piqued your interest in mindfulness, and that you have made a commitment to meditate daily, for 20 minutes.

As for the 20 minutes, it you didn't attain it yet, please be kind to yourself. If you continue on this journey you will reach the 20 minutes. We promise. It just takes some people longer to reach that goal than others.

Reflection No. 1: Pen/pencil time!

Today you are going to write a letter to your six-month-from-now self. Things to include in the letter:
   a. What does mindfulness mean to me today?
   b. The length of time I am meditating and how many days a week?
   c. What do I hope I will be doing with mindfulness six months from now?
   d. Is there anything else I would like to remind my future self about, for example, how I am feeling about mindfulness today?

Set up
- Date the letter.
- Write Dear (fill in your name).
- Write your letter. Sign it in a very kind way.
- Then seal it in an envelope, put a stamp on it, address it to yourself, and give it to someone you can trust to mail it to you six months from now.

Six months from now, when this letter arrives, it will surprise – and we hope, delight you.

Reflection No. 2: Pen/pencil time!

Go back to Day 4 and take the Mindfulness Awareness Survey for the third time. Really pay attention today to your answers. How have you changed?

Are there any areas you think need some work?

Reflection No. 3: No pen/pencil!

Go back and re-read your contract. Commit again. And commit to continue reading it monthly.

No. 56 of 56 Ways

This is the easiest Way so far: Pat yourself on the back for a job well done. You've learned a lot and you need to recognize that you just took an amazing journey, the beginning of a mindful path that will hopefully only get better for you daily.

> **Meditation:** 20 minutes! Forever!

YOUR MINDFULNESS ℞ FOR LIFE

1. Meditate at least 20 minutes each day.
2. Each morning and every night, say "I love you (your name), followed by five deep, slow breaths.
3. In times of stress – and these include the happiest times of your life as well as the not-so-happy – poll your Triangle of Self-Awareness – emotions, thoughts, physical sensations – to see how your body is reacting to the stressor.
4. Journal daily – even on your busiest days. If you only write "Meditated XX number of minutes today," or simply write "Hi!" or "Good night!" it gets you into the habit of reaching for your journal and writing something. The operative word in that last sentence is "habit."

> *Leading a mindful life is a journey not a destination and the Pathway to Mindfulness can take many twists and turns.*
>
> *If you follow these four steps and make them an important part of your daily life, your journey will be a whole lot less bumpy.*

EPILOGUE

> **Don't be afraid of an endless road,
> but the road with an end!**
> —MEHMET MURAT ILDAN,
> TURKISH AUTHOR

TODAY, WE HOPE MANY THINGS for you....

...That you have embraced meditation, making it the most important part of your daily life.

...That you are beginning to live your life in the present moment, taking time to enjoy the little things that once went unnoticed.

...That you took our advice at the end of every week, and re-read your contract, and today you are recommitting to it.

...That you are beginning to respond rather than react to life's issues.

...And finally, that today you fully agree that this is not the end of your mindful journey but just the beginning.

Join us!

We would love to stay in touch with you – and there are various ways you can do that. You can join us on Facebook and Instagram where we share some of Bill's amazing inspirational photographs, the latest research on the benefits of meditation and mindfulness, and our blog posts about topics that will hopefully continue to pique your interest in mindfulness.

If you are really committed to mindfulness, please send us an email at info@PathwayToMindfulness.com to join our mailing list. In turn, we will send you our guide for better sleep. We promise to not bombard you with emails, but we do send out newsletters and information about classes we are leading that you will hopefully find informative.

If you would like to continue your journey with us in person, we see clients in Fairfield County, CT – often in their homes. We also ZOOM with clients all over the world, so that is always an option.

We are wrapping up our next book, Mindful Eating Rx, a mindful approach to eating. On first blush you might think this book is only geared to those wanting to shed pounds, but honestly it is for anyone who wants to enjoy their food more, pay attention to what goes into their bodies and learn how whatever passes your lips – food or beverage – effects your Triangle of Self-Awareness. By the way – if you need to lose weight, you can. We did.

We wish you peace and ease, and a life filled with the ability to be present in life's moments — and weave them into of the story of your life.

Kindly,

Bill and Valerie

ACKNOWLEDGMENTS

We'd like to thank our brilliant clients, who have shared their lives with us over the years and made us better teachers and guides. Without each of them, this journey would not have been as fulfilling as it is.

We need to go back to the beginning and thank Jon Kabat-Zinn, who brought the concept of mindfulness to the Western world. We studied his program at the University of Massachusetts Medical School, Center for Mindfulness, a program that was our initial immersion in the subject of mindfulness. There are hundreds of other mindfulness educators we have studied with over the years, expanding our knowledge, which we in turn pass on to our clients.

Thank you to all the researchers who understand that meditation and mindful living truly can impact lives in innumerable ways. The time and money that has been devoted to this topic is helping so many people live lives where they are free to engage, nourish, explore and thrive – and most importantly – breathe.

Special thanks to our editors, Ann Clark, PhD, Jack Foster, Rev. Sharon Amundsen and Tony Amundsen, who spent hours of their valuable time reading and re-reading our drafts, giving us important information that made the book stronger. To our dedicated client Mike Shullman, who wrote the book's forward and brainstormed ways to make the book a success.

To author Jerry Zezima, who helped us understand the world of self-publishing. To the Self-Publishing School, for their invaluable step-by-step lessons on how to publish and market a book. And finally to our coach, Scott Allan, for his patience in answering our hundreds of questions and his knowledge of the world of self-publishing that put us on the right path.

Finally, thank you to the miracle that is mindfulness. It is a beautiful way to live, in the present with presence.

RESOURCES BY CHAPTER

Addiction

Marianne T. Marcus, EdD, RN, FAAN and Aleksandra Zgierska, MD, PhD, Sinha R. Mindfulness-Based Therapies for Substance Use Disorders: Part 1, The role of stress in addiction relapse. *Current Psychiatry Reports*. 2007;9(5):388–395.

Shapiro SL, et al. Mechanisms of mindfulness, *Journal of Clinical Psychology*. 2006;62(3):373–386.

Teasdale JD, Segal Z, Williams JMG. How does cognitive therapy prevent depressive relapse and why should control (mindfulness) training help? *Behaviour Research and Therapy*. 1995;33:25–39.

Witkiewitz K, Marlatt GA, Walker D. Mindfulness-based relapse prevention for alcohol and substance use disorders, *Journal of Cognitive Psychotherapy*. 2005;19(3):211–228.

Simpson TL, et al. PTSD symptoms, substance abuse, and vipassana meditation among incarcerated individuals, *Journal of Traumatic Stress*. 2007;20(3):239–249.

Mark D. Griffiths PhD, Dr. Edo Shonin and William Van Gordon. Addiction and Mindfulness Can mindfulness be a treatment for behavioral addiction? *Psychology Today,* Feb 24, 2016.

Shonin, E., Van Gordon W., & Griffiths, MD, Mindfulness as a treatment for behavioural addiction, *Journal of Addiction Research and Therapy,* 2014, 5: e122. doi: 10.4172/2155-6105.1000e122.

Shonin, E., Van Gordon W., & Griffiths, MD, Current trends in mindfulness and mental health, *International Journal of Mental Health and Addiction,* 2014. 12, 113-115.

Bowen S, Witkiewitz K, Clifasefi SL, Grow J, Chawla N, Hsu SH, Carroll HA, Harrop E, Collins SE, Lustyk MK, Larimer ME., Relative efficacy of mindfulness-based relapse prevention, standard relapse prevention, and treatment as usual for substance use disorders: a randomized clinical trial, *JAMA Psychiatry* 2014 May;71(5):547-56.

Chiesa A, Serretti A., Are mindfulness-based interventions effective for substance use disorders? A systematic review of the evidence, *University of Bologna,* Bologna, Italy.

ADHD

Zylowska Lidia, The Mindfulness Prescription for Adult ADHD: An 8-Step Program for Strengthening Attention, *Trumpeter; Pap/Com edition,* Feb. 14, 2012.

Bertin, Mark, MD, Mindful Parenting for ADHD: A Guide to Cultivating Calm, Reducing Stress, and Helping Children Thrive, *New Harbinger Publications*; 1 edition, Sept. 1, 2015.

Zylowska, Lidia, Ackerman Deborah L. , Yang, May H., Futrell, Julie L., Horton, Nancy L., Hale, T. Sigi, Pataki, Caroly, Smalley, Susan L. Mindfulness Meditation Training in Adults and Adolescents With ADHD: A Feasibility Study, *Journal of Attention Disorders,* May 2007.

Modesto-Lowe, Vania, Farahmand, Pantea, Chaplin, Margaret and Sarro, Lauren. Does mindfulness meditation improve attention in attention deficit hyperactivity disorder? *World Journal of Psychology*, 2015.

Mitchell, John T. PhD, McIntyre, Elizabeth, MBA, English, Joseph SMA, Dennis, Michelle FBA, Beckham, Jean C. PhD, Kollins, Scott H. PhD, A Pilot Trial of Mindfulness Meditation Training for Attention-Deficit/Hyperactivity Disorder in Adulthood: Impact on Core Symptoms, Executive Functioning, and Emotion Dysregulation, *Journal of Attention Disorder*, 2017 Nov;21(13):1105-1120. doi: 10.1177/1087054713513328.

Linda Harrison, Ramesh Manocha, Katya Rubia, Sahaja Yoga Meditation as a Family Treatment Programme for Children with Attention Deficit-Hyperactivity Disorder, *Clinical Child Psychology and Psychiatry*, 2004.

Anxiety

Vollestad, Nielsen, Mindfulness and acceptance-based interventions for anxiety disorders: A systematic review and meta-analysis, *University of Bergen*, Norway, 2011.

Lu C-F, Smith LN, Gau C-H Exploring the Zen meditation experiences of patients with generalized anxiety disorder: a focus-group approach, *Journal of Nursing*. 2012;20(1):43-51. doi: .1097/JNR.0b013e3182466e83.

Kabat-Zinn, J. *Full Catastrophe Living: Using the Wisdom of Your Body and Mind to Face Stress, Pain, and Illness*, Bantam; Revised, Updated edition September 24, 2013

Hoge EA, Hölzel BK, Marques L, Metcalf CA, Brach N, Lazar SW, Simon NM, Mindfulness and self-compassion in generalized anxiety disorder: examining predictors of disability, *Evidentiary Based Complementary Alternative Medicine*, 2013;2013:576258. doi: 10.1155/2013/576258. Epub 2013 Sep 23.

Hölzel BK, Hoge EA, Greve DN, Gard T, Creswell JD, Brown KW, Barrett LF, Schwartz C, Vaitl D, Lazar SW, Neural mechanisms of symptom improvements in generalized anxiety disorder following mindfulness training, *Neuroimage Clin*. 2013 Mar 25;2:448-58. doi: 10.1016/j.nicl.2013.03.011. eCollection 2013.

Depression

Greenberg J, Datta T, Shapero BG, Sevinc G, Mischoulon D, Lazar SW, Compassionate Hearts Protect Against Wandering Minds: Self-compassion Moderates the Effect of Mind-Wandering on Depression, *Spirituality in Clinical Practice*, 2018 Sep;5(3):155-169. doi: 10.1037/scp0000168.

Insomnia

Black D, PhD, MPH, O'Reilly G, BS, Olmstead R, PhD; Breen E, PhD; Irwin M, MD, Mindfulness Meditation and Improvement in Sleep Quality and Daytime Impairment Among Older Adults With Sleep Disturbances, A Randomized Clinical Trial, *JAMA Internal Medicine* 2015;175(4):494-501. oi:10.1001/jamainternmed.2014.8081

Loneliness

Creswell J, Irwin M, Burklund L, Lieberman M, Arevalo J, Ma J, Crabb Breen E, Cole S, Mindfulness-Based Stress Reduction Training Reduces Loneliness and Pro-Inflammatory Gene Expression in Older Adults: A Small Randomized Controlled Trial, Brain, Behavior, and Immunity, Volume 26, Issue 7, October 2012,

Pain

Zeidan F, Adler-Neal AL, Wells RE, et al., Mindfulness-meditation-based pain relief is not mediated by endogenous opioids, *Journal of Neuroscience.* 2016;36(11):3391-3397.

Gard T, Hölzel BK, Sack AT, Hempel H, Lazar SW, Vaitl D, Ott U, Pain attenuation through mindfulness is associated with decreased cognitive control and increased sensory processing in the brain, *Cerebral Cortex.* 2012, Nov;22(11):2692-702. doi: 10.1093/cercor/bhr352. Epub 2011 Dec 15.

Zeidan, Grant, Brown, McHaffie, Coghilla, Mindfulness meditation-related pain relief: Evidence for unique brain mechanisms in the regulation of pain, *US National Library of Medicine, National Institutes of Health Neuroscience Letter*, 2012 Jun 29;520(2):165-73. doi:10.1016/j.neulet.2012.03.082. Epub 2012 Apr 6. Wake Forest School of Medicine.

Morone N, MD, MS; Greco C, PhD; Moore C, PhD; et al., Chronic Low Back Pain, A Randomized Clinical Trial, *JAMA Intern Medicine*, 2016;176(3):329-337. doi:10.1001/jamainternmed.2015.8033.

PTSD

Vujanovic AA, Niles B, Pietrefesa A, Schmertz SK, Potter CM. Mindfulness in the treatment of posttraumatic stress disorder among military veterans, *Professional Psychology: Research and Practice*, 2011 Feb 1;42(1):24-31.

Boyd J, MSc, Lanius R, MD, PhD, McKinnon M, PhD, Mindfulness-based treatments for posttraumatic stress disorder: a review of the treatment literature and neurobiological evidence, *Journal of Psychiatry and Neuroscience*, 2018 Jan; 43(1): 7–25.

King AP, Block SR, Sripada RK, Rauch S, Giardino N, Favorite T, Angstadt M, Kessler D, Welsh R, Liberzon I, Altered Default Mode Network (DMN) Resting State Functional Connectivity Following

Mindfulness-Based Exposure Therapy for Posttraumatic Stress Disorder (PTSD) In Combat Veterans Of Afghanistan and Iraq, *Journal of Psychiatry and Neuroscience*, 2017 Oct 3. doi: 10.1503/jpn.170021.

Mindfulness Meditation Therapy for PTSD, Peter Strong, PhD, www.mentalhelp.net/blogs/mindfulness-meditation-therapy-for-ptsd/

Davis L, MD, Whetsell C, PhD, Hamner M, MD, Carmody J, PhD, Rothbaum B, PhD, Allen S, PhD, A.B.P.P., Bartolucci A , PhD, Southwick S, MD, Bremner JD, MD, A Multisite Randomized Controlled Trial of Mindfulness-Based Stress Reduction in the Treatment of Posttraumatic Stress Disorder, *Psychiatric Research and Clinical Practice*, Sept. 2018https://doi.org/10.1176/appi.prcp.20180002.

Bremner JD, Mishra S, Campanella C, Shah M, Kasher N, Evans S, Fani N, Shah AJ, Reiff C, Davis LL, Vaccarino V, Carmody J., A Pilot Study of the Effects of Mindfulness-Based Stress Reduction on Post-traumatic Stress Disorder Symptoms and Brain Response to Traumatic Reminders of Combat in Operation Enduring Freedom/Operation Iraqi Freedom Combat Veterans with Post-traumatic Stress Disorder, Depression and Anxiety 33:289–299 2016.

Polusny MA, Erbes CR, Thuras P, Moran A, Lamberty GJ, Collins RC, Rodman JL, Lim KO. Mindfulness-Based Stress Reduction for Posttraumatic Stress Disorder Among Veterans: A Randomized Clinical Trial, Minneapolis Veterans Affairs Health Care System, Minneapolis, Minn., *JAMA*. 2015;314(5):456-465. doi:10.1001/jama.2015.8361.

Simpson TL, et al. PTSD symptoms, substance abuse, and vipassana meditation among incarcerated individuals, *Journal of Traumatic Stress*. 2007;20(3):239–249.

Kearney D, Malte C, McManus C, Martinez M, Felleman B, Simpson S,. Loving-Kindness Meditation for Posttraumatic Stress Disorder: A Pilot Study, *Journal of Trauma Stress*. 2013 Aug;26(4):426-34. doi: 10.1002/jts.2183225.

Linder J, What Is Trauma, and Can Mindfulness Help Treat It? How do mindfulness and trauma relate? Here's what you need to know, *Psychology Today,* Sept. 19, 2019.

Stress

Goyal M, MD, MPH; Singh S, MD, MPH; Sibinga E, MD, MHS; Gould N, PhD; Rowland-Seymour A, MD; Sharma R, BSc; Berger Z, MD, PhD; Sleicher D, MS, MPH; Maron D, MHS; Shihab M, MBChB, MPH; Ranasinghe P, MD, MPH; Linn S, BA; Saha S, MD; Bass E, MD, MPH; Haythornthwaite J, PhD,. Meditation Programs for Psychological Stress and Well-being, A Systematic Review and Meta-analysis, The Johns Hopkins University, Baltimore, Maryland, *JAMA Intern Medicine.* 2014;174(3):357-368. doi:10.1001/jamainternmed.2013.13018.

Lazar SW, Bush G, Gollub RL, Fricchione GL, Khalsa G, Benson H. Functional brain mapping of the relaxation response and meditation, *Neuroreport.* 2000 May 15;11(7):1581-5.

Hölzel BK, Carmody J, Evans KC, Hoge EA, Dusek JA, Morgan L, Pitman RK, Lazar SW, Stress reduction correlates with structural changes in the amygdala, *Social Cognitive and Affective Neuroscience.* 2010 Mar;5(1):11-7. doi: 10.1093/scan/nsp034. Epub 2009 Sep 23.

Beddoe A, Murphy S, Does Mindfulness Decrease Stress and Foster Empathy Among Nursing Student? 2004. *Journal of Nursing Education,* 43(7), 305-312.

Day 10: Strengthen your brain

Daniel Siegel, MD, Mindsight: The New Science of Personal Transformation, Bantam, Nov. 30, 2009

Hölzel BK, Carmody J, Vangel M, Congleton C, Yerramsetti SM, Gard T, Lazar SW, Mindfulness practice leads to increases in regional brain gray matter density, *Psychiatry Research*, 2011 Jan 30;191(1):36-43. doi: 10.1016/j.pscychresns.2010.08.006.

Lazar SW, Kerr CE, Wasserman RH, Gray JR, Greve DN, Treadway MT, McGarvey M, Quinn BT, Dusek JA, Benson H, Rauch SL, Moore CI, Fischl B, Meditation experience is associated with increased cortical thickness, *Neuroreport*, 2005, Nov. 28;16(17):1893-7.

Hölzel BK, Carmody J, Evans KC, Hoge EA, Dusek JA, Morgan L, Pitman RK, Lazar SW, Stress reduction correlates with structural changes in the amygdala. *Social Cognitive and Affective Neuroscience*, 2010 Mar;5(1):11-7. doi: 10.1093/scan/nsp034. Epub 2009 Sep 23.

Kerr CE, Jones SR, Wan Q, Pritchett DL, Wasserman RH, Wexler A, Villanueva JJ, Shaw JR, Lazar SW, Kaptchuk TJ, Littenberg R, Hämäläinen MS, Moore CI., Effects of mindfulness meditation training on anticipatory alpha modulation in primary somatosensory cortex, *Brain Research Bulletin*. 2011 May 30;85(3-4):96-103. doi: 10.1016/j.brainresbull.2011.03.026. Epub 2011 Apr 8.

Singleton O, Hölzel BK, Vangel M, Brach N, Carmody J, Lazar SW. Change in Brainstem Gray Matter Concentration Following a Mindfulness-Based Intervention is Correlated with Improvement in Psychological Well-Being, *Frontiers in Human Neuroscience*. 2014 Feb 18;8:33. doi: 10.3389/fnhum.2014.00033. eCollection 2014.

Hölzel BK, Lazar SW, Gard T, Schuman-Olivier Z, Vago DR, Ott U, How Does Mindfulness Meditation Work? Proposing Mechanisms of Action from a Conceptual and Neural Perspective, *Perspectives on Psychological Science*. 2011 Nov;6(6):537-59. doi: 10.1177/1745691611419671.

Brewer J, Worhunsky P, Gray J, Tang Y, Weber J, Kober H. Meditation experience is associated with differences in default mode network activity and connectivity *PNAS*, Dec. 13, 2011 108 (50) 20254-20259; https://doi.org/10.1073/pnas.1112029108.

Greenberg J, Romero VL, Elkin-Frankston S, Bezdek MA, Schumacher EH, Lazar SW, Reduced interference in working memory following mindfulness training is associated with increases in hippocampal volume, *Brain Imaging Behavior*. 2019 Apr;13(2):366-376. doi: 10.1007/s11682-018-9858-4.

Fox KC, Nijeboer S, Dixon ML, Floman JL, Ellamil M, Rumak SP, Sedlmeier P, Christoff K, Is meditation associated with altered brain structure? A systematic review and meta-analysis of morphometric neuroimaging in meditation practitioners, *Neuroscience Biobehavioral Re*view, 2014 Jun;43:48-73. doi: 10.1016/j.neubiorev.2014.03.016. Epub 2014 Apr 3.

Tang YY, Hölzel BK, Posner MI The Neuroscience of mindfulness meditation, *Nature Reviews Neuroscience*. 2015 Apr;16(4):213-25. doi: 10.1038/nrn3916. Epub 2015 Mar 18.

Aging

Gard T, Taquet M, Dixit R, Hölzel BK, de Montjoye YA, Brach N, Salat DH, Dickerson BC, Gray JR, Lazar SW.

Fluid intelligence and brain functional organization in aging yoga and meditation practitioners, *Frontiers in Aging Neuroscience*. 2014 Apr 22;6:76. doi: 10.3389/fnagi.2014.00076.

Gard T, Taquet M, Dixit R, Hölzel BK, Dickerson BC, Lazar SW. Greater widespread functional connectivity of the caudate in older adults who practice kripalu yoga and vipassana meditation than in controls, *Frontiers in Human Neuroscience*. 2015 Mar 16;9:137. doi: 10.3389/fnhum.2015.00137.

Santaella DF, Balardin JB, Afonso RF, Giorjiani GM, Sato JR, Lacerda SS, Amaro E Jr, Lazar S, Kozasa EH.

Greater Anteroposterior Default Mode Network Functional Connectivity in Long-Term Elderly Yoga Practitioners, *Frontiers in Aging Neuroscience*, 2019 Jul 2;11:158. doi: 10.3389/fnagi.2019.00158.

Gard T, Hölzel BK, Lazar SW., The potential effects of meditation on age-related cognitive decline: a systematic review, *Annals of the NY Academy of Sciences*. 2014 Jan;1307:89-103. doi: 10.1111/nyas.12348. Review.

Day 11: Your body on stress

Jansen AS1, Nguyen XV, Karpitskiy V, Mettenleiter TC, Loewy AD, Central command neurons of the sympathetic nervous system: basis of the fight-or-flight response, *Science* 1995 Oct 27;270(5236):644-6.

Understanding the stress response. Chronic activation of this survival mechanism impairs health, *Harvard Health Publishing*, Harvard Medical School, May 2018.

Kabat-Zinn, J. Full Catastrophe Living: Using the Wisdom of Your Body and Mind to Face Stress, Pain, and Illness, *Bantam*; Revised, Updated edition (September 24, 2013).

Fight or Flight Response *Encyclopedia Brittianica* www.britannica.com/science/fight-or-flight-response.

Fight or Flight, *Wikipedia* en.wikipedia.org/wiki/Fight-or-flight_response

The Science of Stress. faculty.weber.edu/molpin/healthclasses/1110/bookchapters/stressphysiologychapter.htm.

Day 13: The pleasant and not-so-pleasant

Lamia M, PhD, Emotional Memories: When People and Events Remain with You, Recalling the past can awaken an emotional response. *Psychology Today,* https://www.psychologytoday.com/us/blog/intense-and-strong-feelings/201203/emotional-memories-when-people-and-events-remain March 06, 2012.

Cassano J, The Science of Why You Should Spend Your Money on Experiences, Not Things, Fast Company, www.fastcompany.com/3043858/the-science-of-why-you-should-spend-your-money-on-experiences-not-thing.

Day 15: The happy quotient

Mark Stibich, PhD, The Benefits of Positive Thinking and Happiness, www.verywellmind.com/accentuate-the-positive-positive-thinking-and-happiness-2224115.

Day 18: Your breath

Medina J, MD. *Brain Rules*, Pear Press.

Day 20: Changing behaviors

Jon Kabat-Zinn, STOP meditation.

Day 25: What about them goldfish!

McSpadden K, You Now Have a Shorter Attention Span Than a Goldfish, Time, time.com/3858309/attention-spans-goldfish.

Day 27: By the sea....

G. Alan Marlatt, PhD, Urge Surfing.

Day 30: Inner critic part 2

Rick Hanson, PhD.

Day 34: Body scan

University of Massachusetts, Center for Mindfulness.

Day 37: The vagus nerve

Fredrickson B, Cohn M, Coffey K, Pek J, and Finkel S, Open Hearts Build Lives: Positive Emotions, Induced Through Loving-Kindness Meditation, Build Consequential Personal Resources, *Journal of Personality and Social Psychology*, 2008.

Seppala E PhD, 18 Science-Based Reasons to Try Loving-Kindness Meditation Today! *Psychology Today,* emmaseppala.com/18-science-based-reasons-try-loving-kindness-meditation-today, Sept. 2014.

Kok BE, Fredrickson BL,. Upward spirals of the heart: autonomic flexibility, as indexed by vagal tone, reciprocally and prospectively predicts positive emotions and social connectedness, *Biological Psychology*. 2010 Dec;85(3):432-6. doi: 10.1016/j.biopsycho.2010.09.005. Epub 2010 Sep 22.

Day 44: Make stress your friend

Keller A, Litzelman K, Wisk L, Maddox T, Cheng E, Creswell P, Witt W., University of Wisconsin – Madison, Does the Perception That Stress Affects Health Matter? The Association with Health and Mortality, *Health Psychology Journal,* 2012 Sep;31(5):677-84. doi: 10.1037/a0026743.

Day 47: Equanimity

Desbordes G, Gard T, Hoge EA, Hölzel BK, Kerr C, Lazar SW, Olendzki A, Vago DR., Moving beyond Mindfulness: Defining Equanimity as an Outcome Measure in Meditation and Contemplative Research, *Mindfulness* (N Y). 2014 Jan 21;2014, doi: 10.1007/s12671-013-0269-8.

Day 48: Gratitude

Lyubomirsky S, Dickerhoof R, Boehm J, and Sheldon K, Becoming Happier Takes Both a Will and a Proper Way: An Experimental Longitudinal Intervention to Boost Well-Being, Emotion, *American Psychological Association* 2011, Vol. 11, No. 2, 391–402 1528-3542/11

Sheldon K, Lyubomirsky S, How to increase and sustain positive emotion: The effects of expressing gratitude and visualizing best possible selves, *The Journal of Positive Psychology*, Volume 1, 2006 - Issue 2: Positive Emotions.

Lin C, Yeh Y, How Gratitude Influences Well-Being: A Structural Equation Modeling Approach, *Social Indicators Research*, August 2014.

In Praise of Gratitude, Harvard Medical School, *Harvard Health Publishing*, www.health.harvard.edu/mind-and-mood/in-praise-of-gratitude University of California at Berkeley, *greatergood.Berkeley.edu.*

Day 52: Awe and wonder

Stellar JE, John-Henderson N, Anderson CL, Gordon AM, McNeil GD, Keltner D, Positive affect and markers of inflammation: discrete positive emotions predict lower levels of inflammatory cytokines, *Emotion.* 2015 Apr;15(2):129-33. doi: 10.1037/emo0000033. Epub 2015 Jan 19.

Day 53: How to say "*no*"

www.verywell .com

ABOUT THE AUTHORS

VALERIE FOSTER WAS A JOURNALIST, a field rife with constant pressures and deadlines. She has studied many forms of meditation, and a decade ago focused on insight mindfulness meditation, a practice that enters every facet of her daily life – both personal and professional. She wishes she had found this meditation style years ago, but because of mindfulness, doesn't look back and is just so thankful she has it now.

Bill Van Ollefen was as a corporate executive, working all over the globe, until a spinal cord injury caused the worst kind of neurological pain imaginable – the type that often leads to suicide, which he considered often. He turned to insight mindfulness meditation and the effects have been profound. As his practice deepened, his experience with pain evolved. His pain continues to increase, although today it doesn't rule his life, he doesn't suffer, and he is happy, thriving and looking forward to a long life.

They own Pathway to Mindfulness and have helped hundreds of clients live happier, healthier, more focused lives. Both studied Mindfulness-Based Stress Reduction at the University of Massachusetts Medical School, Center for Mindfulness, vipassana meditation at the University of Holistic Theology, and are certified meditation instructors, mindfulness life coaches, cognitive behavioral therapy (CBT) practitioners, CBT life coaches/anxiety specialty and mindfulness CBT practitioners. They are also certified Am I Hungry? teachers.

Made in the USA
Middletown, DE
02 July 2020